PYOTR

The Life and Music of Pyotr Ilyich Tchaikovsky

STEVE MORETTI
PAUL VAN GELDROP

READER COMMENTS

"Pyotr Ilyich Tchaikovsky - a brilliant composer tormented by self-doubt. This is a sensitive evocation of the life of this troubled genius, from childhood to his untimely death. I thoroughly recommend this book. Read it and discover - or rediscover - Tchaikovsky the man and his wonderful music." - *Marise Moland-Chapman*

"Learn not only about the hauntingly beautiful music Pyotr Tchaikovsky gave the world, but also about the idealistic young man who crafted that music. A young man growing to adulthood in an era that held very rigid standards about how life should be lived; Pyotr wrestled with an overbearing mother, insufficient funds, angst and indecision regarding his personal life choices." - *Lady Anne*

"I have never given classical music and thought before but while reading this heart touching story I had a change of heart. I have not only learned more about musical history and rules I was inspired to listen to some of the musical pieces I read about. Thank you for such a wonderful book." - *Nevine Ramirez*

"I am almost completely musically illiterate, but even I could understand Paul van Geldrop's explanations. His sections will be much appreciated by those who want to understand the nuts and bolts of composition. You brought Pyotr Tchaikovsky to life. It certainly comes through loud and clear what a tortured soul he was. You made me cry with your ending. Bravo!" - *Marti Panniker*

"I teared up reading the last chapter and epilogue of Pyotr! I hate getting emotional in public. (I was waiting for my husband while he was in with the dentist.) I was really wrapped up in the story and can't imagine the works that we've missed out on due to that incredibly talented life cut short by cholera." - *Diane Craig*

How often does a reader get the chance to not only read a captivating book about a well known composer (in this case Tchaikovsky) but also get to learn about musical history through the ages as well as the art of musical composition? Moretti gives us that opportunity in his newest book, Pytor. You'll be amazed at the things about music that make it what it is today and the man that gave us so many treasures like 'The Nutcracker' and 'Swan Lake. - *Trulyn Bermis*

A FREE BOOK FOR YOU

Katharine Carnegie's passion is her music, but she is lost for words to complete it in 1745 Scotland. Adeena Stuart is a rebellious teenage musician in 2003. While Katharine must decide which brother she supports in the uprising against England, Adeena and her psychic grandmother glimpse the past calling out to the present.

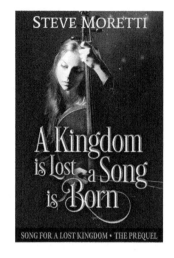

In this Prequel to the best-selling *Song for a Lost Kingdom* series, the origins of the story unfold as the Scottish parliament votes itself out of existence in on January 7, 1707.

The prequel also includes the first four chapters of **Music is Not Bound by Time,** Book I of the *Song for a Lost Kingdom* series.

Download your free copy of *A Kingdom is Lost, a Song is Born'* from my website: **stevemoretti.ca** and we will also send you a link to download a free audiobook version of the book when you join my mailing list.

CONTENTS

Pyotr

The Life and Music of Pyotr Ilyich Tchaikovsky
by Steve Moretti and Paul van Geldrop

Copyright © 2021 Steve Moretti, Paul van Geldrop
All rights reserved.
Editor: Lara Clouden
Copy Editor: S. Daisy

Published by DWA Media
OTTAWA • CANADA

DWA Media
PO 493, Richmond, Ontario K0A 2Z0
https://www.stevemoretti.ca/

FOREWORD

His life was a study in the art of contradiction.

Pyotr Tchaikovsky was deeply affected by the women in his life – those he loved, those he despised, and those whose affection he longed so badly to hold.

Yet, aside from music, his truest passion was reserved for men.

Pyotr had an intense patriotism for his homeland. But his profound relationship with the country of his birth did not come to fruition until he finally left Russia.

He wrote some of the most delicate, sensual, and romantic music ever composed, and yet his 1812 overture is among the loudest pieces of classical music ever performed. And it is perhaps the only one that includes a cannon as a percussion instrument.

In death, Tchaikovsky was celebrated as one of the most gifted voices of classical music, yet the details of his personal life were sublimated for years. To this day, his homosexuality is still denied amongst official circles in the country of his birth, even though he is almost a folk hero to Mother Russia.

Perhaps it is only by commemorating the music he created, the reflection of human emotion – from profound sorrow to magical wonder – that we can truly understand the timeless conflicts that are Pyotr Ilyich Tchaikovsky.

About this book

Pytor - The Life and Music Pyotr Ilyich Tchaikovsky is really two books in one.

The odd numbered chapters are dramatized scenes of his life (all crap') written by historical fiction author Steve Moretti. The even numbered chapters are a layman's guide to Tchaikovsky's music and influences by composer Paul van Geldrop. emphasis on 'layman' but o.k.

Together, they provide a comprehensive analysis of both the (I s don't think so) man and his music. While some liberties were taken with dramatized sections, the key details are drawn from letters, and accounts by Tchaikovsky's contemporaries including his brother Modest.

You may prefer to read either the even or odd numbered chapters in isolation from each other, or in the sequence presented here. Either way, we do hope you enjoy this portrait of a gifted musician and the legacy he left behind.

The upcoming audiobook version provides additional insights including of course, Pyotr's music, which is central to a full understanding of the man.

For Frank

"In daily intercourse we all loved him, because we felt he loved us in return. His sensibility was extreme, therefore I had to be very careful how I treated him. A trifle wounded him deeply. He was brittle as porcelain."

Fanny Dürbach
Tchaikovsky's childhood governess

CHAPTER 1

VOTKINSK, RUSSIA: 1847 (AGE 7)

Pyotr rubbed his hands together as hard as he could, hoping that maybe it would calm him a little. He did not want to tremble like a silly girl when it was his turn to perform. The cuts on his hands had almost healed, but one deep scar remained. He clenched his fists wishing the wound could somehow magically vanish. *what a load of old kosh!*

It was before he had a keyboard or a piano teacher or any way to make music, that he had cut his hand so deeply. He was searching for sounds, musical notes like the ones he heard on the orchestrion organ that Papa played sometimes. Pyotr had tapped on the windowpane in the kitchen, listening to the dull sound of his finger tapping the glass.

He tapped a little harder and reached higher. Then he pounded even harder. It was not the sound he wanted. He reached lower and pounded fiercely, over and over, until suddenly the window shattered. He screamed in pain, blood pouring from the gash in his hand, dripping onto the polished kitchen floor.

"Mama!" he cried. "Mama! Please, help me!"

But she was not at home and it was Papa who bandaged his hands that night and said 'yes, yes,' they would find a music tutor and 'yes', she would show him all the notes and 'of course' he could practice every day. *tosh continued*

Now here he was on his seventh birthday, getting set to perform after practicing for so long. He had dreamed about this party for almost a week. *are you sure it wasn't a fortnight?* It was Papa's idea, to celebrate Pyotr's birthday. All the children would play for the special guests who had been invited; Fanny, his beautiful and perfect governess, Maria his wonderful music tutor and Jakub, Papa's handsome army friend from far away Poland.

Pyotr watched his sister Sasha at the piano as she began to play the music she had struggled with all week – *Zerlina's Aria* by Wolfgang Mozart. The music teased his ears, and exploded in his head with its raw beauty. Sasha played it much too quickly, and she hit at least two wrong notes. No matter, even she could not damage music as perfect as this.

When Sasha was done, she stood up and bowed. The guests clapped and cheered. Pyotr was delighted, but Mama did not seem happy. What had displeased her?

"And now," his tutor Maria announced, rising from her chair, "Aleksandra, our precious 'Sasha', and Master Pyotr Ilyich have a surprise for their Mama, Madam Tchaikovsky!" She motioned for Pyotr. He stepped beside Sasha and felt his face turn red. It was on fire. He was much too frightened to play, even though he tried to be brave for such honoured guests.

He caught Fanny's eye. She smiled and blew him a kiss. Oh, that he could kiss her right now on those beautiful lips. She waved her hand for him to take his place and she blew him another kiss. He glowed in the warmth of her face, and her smile and... *How do you know this?! What crap!*

"Pyotr!" his mother's stern whisper cut his daydream short. She looked at him coldly and tilted her head towards the piano. He shivered, turned around and took his place on the bench beside his sister. They placed their hands on the keys, waiting for instructions to begin.

"Please open your ears and your hearts, for the world

premiere of 'Our Mama in Petersburg' by Pyotr and Aleksandra Tchaikovsky," Maria announced in a very big voice for such a tiny room.

Together, Pyotr and Sasha began to play. He felt embarrassed by the simplicity of the song, the first one he had ever tried to make. It must surely be the most horrible music ever written. As they played, he decided he would run and hide as soon as they were finished. Sasha smiled and bounced up and down, nearly knocking him off the bench. This was just a silly game to her.

Mercifully, it was soon over. Everyone clapped again and cheered loudly. Papa even whistled. Pyotr turned around and saw that Mama had no expression whatsoever on her face. He tried to catch her eye, but she turned to Papa and said something to him. She rose stiffly and left the parlour.

Pyotr wanted to shrivel up. If he could simply melt, like ice under the hot Russian sun and quietly flow down the sewer by their house, he would happily do so. He felt his eyes growing wet. He tried to dry them, mad at himself for thinking he could write music like Mozart.

"Pyotr, that was very lovely," a deep voice proclaimed.

It was Jakub, father's friend from far away Poland. Fanny stood next to him and both of them beamed. Mama was gone and Papa had hurried away after her.

"Thank you, sir," Pyotr replied stiffly. "But you must think my music quite silly. I know it is very awful."

"Nonsense!" Jakub replied. He sat down next to Pyotr on the piano bench. "I thought it most delightful." His fingers touched the keyboard, and he played the first bar of 'Our Mama in Petersburg' and then added a flourish and a dramatic ending. "There you go. I just played my first Tchaikovsky!"

Pyotr stared with amazement, his heart pounding in his ears.

"Now, let me show you something else you might enjoy," Jakub continued. "This is a new mazurka by Frédéric Chopin. He is Polish, like me."

Fanny leaned over and whispered, "Happy Birthday, Pyotr!"

She hugged him warmly. As she walked away, Jakub began to play such lively and joyous music as had ever been made on the old family piano. Pyotr sat still listening, seeing the notes as pictures in his head while Jakub performed on the bench beside him.

"You like?" Jakub grinned as he finished.

"Very much, sir," Pyotr replied. "May I try?"

"Please do!"

Pyotr placed his hands on the keys and closed his eyes. He paused a few seconds and then began to play the mazurka, hoping to find the joy that Chopin must have felt composing this. Pyotr could hear the music inside of him, and let it pour out through his fingers, tentative at first and then gaining confidence, until he finished smartly and bowed his head.

"Pyotr!" Jakub exclaimed. "That was... simply extraordinary!" He leaned over and kissed Pyotr on both cheeks and then excitedly, right on the lips. "You have done Master Chopin very, very proud!"

Pyotr stared in wonder and let tears stream freely down his face. This was the best birthday party he could ever remember.

SAINT PETERSBURG: 1850 (AGE 10)

WITH A GREAT GRUNTING EFFORT, THE COACHMAN LIFTED THE last bag to the very top of the carriage. His mother shouted to the driver that they needed to leave with all due haste before the rain became too heavy for the horses.

Pyotr watched as Mama lifted little Sasha up and into the carriage. Sasha waved madly once she found her seat and he smiled back at his darling sister. He didn't want to show her the numbing dread growing inside him. In a few moments Mama and Sasha, and his grown-up stepsister Zina, would leave him in Petersburg.

Alone.

Alone, with no family, save for Modest Alekseyevich, who would be his guardian while he attended school here in Petersburg, so very, very far away from home in Votkinsk.

"Pyotr," his Mama said firmly, as she pulled her leather gloves down and straightened her coat, "you will be a good student. You will study hard and you will do as your guardian requests of you. And you will do it all with a humble attitude."

"Yes, Mama," Pyotr replied. "Of course I will, but..." His ten-year-old eyes were wet, even as he fought to blink the tears away. "Do you... do you have to leave me here, alone?"

His mother leaned down and held his chin. She wiped his eyes and kissed him quickly. "You are almost a man now, Pyotr. It is time for you to act like a man."

She stood up and bowed her head to Modest Alekseyevich. "Thank you again for looking after Pyotr. He is a good boy, but sometimes..." she hesitated a moment, studying Pyotr with a frown, "sometimes he is much too delicate in his manner. I hope you can help him to grow up, not behave like such a child."

Modest nodded. "Do not worry about him. He will be like another son for me."

Mama touched Pyotr's head, held it a second and walked away without another word. She climbed into the carriage with Sasha and Zina, then called out to the coachman. The driver acknowledged her with a loud crack of the whip and the two horses, glistening in the light rain, began to pull the carriage away.

Pyotr watched it begin to move as the hooves of the horses clattered lightly on the stones.

"No!" he cried. "No, no, no!"

Modest Alekseyevich reached for him, but Pyotr pulled away from his grip. As the carriage rolled slowly down the lane, he ran behind, desperate to find a way to stop it. They could not leave him alone, deserted like this from Mama and Papa, and from all his brothers and sisters.

He would die of loneliness here. He must stop them. Must beg Mama not to go, not to leave him.

"Mama!" he yelled as he ran after the carriage. The startled coachman turned toward him and their eyes met.

Mama peered out from the carriage. "*Nyet!*" She tried to wave him off, but Pyotr kept running until finally he caught up and grabbed first at the footboard, then the splashboard, and was dragged along until he lost his grip and fell onto the muddy lane.

He lay dazed in the mud a moment, staring at the carriage, which had stopped. His mother peered out at him. He picked himself up and ran toward her, but the carriage had already started to roll down the lane. Pyotr ran after it and desperately threw himself against one of the large wheels of the moving vehicle which suddenly stopped as the driver pulled back hard on the reins.

He held the wheel and cried out in despair, "Mama! Don't leave me!"

Her head poked out of the carriage. She looked at him sternly. "You are not a boy anymore, Pyotr."

With that she motioned with her arm for the coachmen to proceed. He nodded and cracked his whip once more. As the carriage began to move, Pyotr felt himself being lifted off the wheels by strong arms. Modest held him tightly as the coach rolled away.

Pyotr felt his chest tighten. He fought for breath and began to shiver as he watched the coach disappear down the muddy, cobblestone lane into the misty morning rain.

"IT'S A *FRICTION MATCH*," ANATOLY EXPLAINED AS PYOTR watched in wonder. His new friend at the Schmelling school struck a small stick against a piece of coarse paper and *voila*, a tiny flame erupted. Anatoly used it to light the thin cigarette he produced clandestinely from the pocket of his blazer.

After a few puffs, he passed the lit cigarette to Pyotr who eagerly accepted it and placed it to his lips.

"Just inhale," Anatoly explained. "You might cough a little, but let it work its way inside you. It will refresh you."

Pyotr sucked the little rolled paper filled with sweet tobacco. At first it bit his throat and he almost gagged, but he was determined to ingest the smoke like Anatoly, the only friend he had in this school, and the only boy who seemed to believe whatever Pyotr told him.

After a few drags, he passed the burning cigarette back. "Last night I heard the sound again, musical sounds following me into my sleep and when I awoke, they came and followed me to school this morning."

Anatoly stared back as he took a deep suck on the cigarette. The tip of it glowed brightly, as if in satisfaction at Pyotr's story. "Do you ever write them down?" Anatoly asked. "These musical sounds? You know I would love to know what they sound like..."

"*Prekati eto!*" The sharp voice of the school inspector, Colonel Rutenberg, startled the boys.

"Stop what?" Anatoly shot back, flinging the lit cigarette under the bench and stepping on it.

Colonel Rutenberg bent over, yanked Anatoly's foot away and picked up the smouldering remains of the cigarette. "Trying to fool me?" the Colonel intoned darkly. He crushed the cigarette and threw it into the boy's face. "Come with me. Now!"

Anatoly stood up, head held high, and walked towards the school's back entrance as Pyotr watched in alarm and then followed, keeping his eyes lowered to the ground.

Inside the classroom, the Colonel ordered Anatoly to the front of the room. "Your fiendish classmate was caught smoking *and* lying," the Colonel boomed to the twenty-three young boys, the oldest of whom had only last week celebrated his eleventh birthday.

"For that, he is sentenced to sixty-five strokes, by my own hand." Colonel Rutenberg paused a moment as a collective gasp rose from the boys. "Then each of you will feel the whip, to teach you how it might feel upon your own backside, if you too choose to disobey the rules."

Anatoly, silent and brave to this point, cowered on his knees. "Please, sir. I am stupid and I erred in judgement. Please, have mercy!" His eyes were wet.

"Strip!" the Colonel shouted. "You made your choices. Now remove all your clothing, and lay yourself across this bench." He dragged it closer to where Anatoly remained kneeling. "Now!"

Shaking, shivering and sobbing, Anatoly removed his trousers and his shirt. He stood, looking sheepish in his boxers and black socks.

"I said *all* your clothing," the Colonel grunted. "Unless you want another twenty lashes."

Anatoly flinched. "No, sir. No!" He removed his socks and then turned around and removed his boxers. Pyotr stared from his seat, his heart was pounding like a cannon firing over and over in his chest. He was not sure he could watch much more without passing out.

Anatoly lay himself prostrate over the bench. His naked bottom was exposed as he awaited his punishment. Colonel Rutenberg gathered the leather switch in hand. "Let each kiss of the whip remind you of your duty to Schmelling, to Russia, to your classmates, and... to me!"

With that, he snapped the leather rod across Anatoly's exposed buttocks. The boy yelped sharply and Pyotr thought he could feel the leather rod himself. Another lash, and another and another... until both Anatoly and Pyotr were sobbing through muffled screams.

With each loud crack of the switch against bare flesh, Pyotr felt wounded, ashamed and afraid. When it was over, Anatoly lay writhing on the ground, naked and curled in a ball. The other boys lined up and one by one, exposed their bare bottom and received five sharp, burning lashes.

As Pyotr felt the pain bite into him for his first lash, he

thought he might die. When the last one struck his body, he cried out in one final sob and let the sound of sorrow echo deep within him to the darkest corners of his heart.

VOTKINSK 1854 (AGE 14)

HIS SISTER SASHA CAREFULLY COVERED THE SMOKY MIRROR IN the parlour with a long black cloth, casting Pyotr's reflection into darkness. He knew the mirror was a gateway to the land of the dead. He was not afraid that if he was the first person to see his image after Mama died he would be next.

This was not her night to die.

"Pyotr," his father whispered. "The clocks, will you please..." His words trailed off.

"No, Papa," Pyotr said softly. "She is stronger than the cholera."

His father's face sagged. He released a deep, hollow moan – a sound more sorrowful than the saddest chord Pyotr had ever heard played on any instrument.

"But if her time *is* tonight," his father rasped, "you must stop the clocks."

"Why, Papa?"

"To help her soul pass..."

Before his father could finish, a tall figure in a black cassock approached. His long hair and beard were untrimmed and untamed. The gold cross around his neck glinted, and the wide *kamilavka* on his head cast a towering shadow on the wall, filling Pyotr with a sense of foreboding.

"You must come with me now," the hieromonk priest said in a dark, glottal tone like gravel grinding in tar.

The hieromonk bowed his head, turned, and marched slowly toward the bedroom chamber where Pyotr knew his mother rested. He followed the priest and his father into the dimly lit chamber. A single candle flickered low on the nightstand.

"Pyotr?" a weak voice called out.

His mother lay tiny and frail in the middle of the bed. At but fourteen years old, Pyotr knew more of this horrible disease than he cared to ever know. The cholera left its victims withered up, shrivelled – and dead.

"Mama," he cried, from his place beside the bed. "I am here. You must be strong."

He raised a hand toward her face, but his father stopped him, slowly lowering Pyotr's hand. "No," he whispered, "you cannot touch her."

The hieromonk leaned over the bed. His beard was so long it touched the sheets drawn over Pyotr's mother. "I will hear your confession now."

There was no response to the request. Pyotr waited anxiously, hoping his mother would rise up from her bed and cast away forever any doubt that she would leave this world. He glanced back at his sister Sasha and his brothers Anatoly and Modest who stood in the shadows weeping quietly, their heads bowed in resignation.

"Confess your sins," the priest repeated, "so you can receive the *Viaticum,* your last Holy Communion."

There was only silence in response to the hieromonk's demand, save the quiet sobbing of the children that filled the dark, tiny chamber with an eerie harmony. Pyotr could not help but join them as his chest tightened and the beating of his heart joined the chorus of hurt.

"I ..." a hollow voice from the bed whispered, "have..."

Everyone in the room listened in reverent silence for Mama to complete her confession. Finally, with a tiny gasp she added, "...sinned."

The clock ticked relentlessly between each effort to expel those three simple words.

"Your sins are forgiven Alexandra Andreievna," the preist replied, making the sign of the cross.

Everyone followed his lead as he continued. "The Lamb of God, who takes away the sins of the world, is with you tonight. Happy are those who are called to His supper."

He took a small piece of crust and held it up. *"Corpus Christi,"* he sang in a chant that seared Pyotr's ears. "The Body of Christ," the priest repeated, moving his hand closer to Alexandra's lips, and touching them with the tiny morsel of bread.

Her mouth opened ever so slightly to his touch. The hieromonk pushed the Eucharist into her mouth.

Pyotr could barely see her face through his tears. "Mama!" he cried, leaning closer. Her eyes opened a second and looked right through him as she passed from this world forever.

What sentimental crap!

THE DARK INK FROM HIS DELICATE PEN GATHERED AT THE NIB in a menacing blob.

Pyotr stared as it grew larger and larger until it finally fell onto a blank sheet of parchment paper, splattering like black blood on ice. He closed his eyes, seeing his mother's face staring at him, even four months after that wretched night in June.

His head sagged. He shivered under the late October chill seeping into his dormitory room. The trees outside were nearly naked now, shedding their leaves even more profusely than the tears he still spilled for her nearly every day.

"Pyotr," he scolded himself, "you need to write to Fanny Dürbach. Tell her that Mama is gone."

He placed the tip of his pen on the parchment, stained with the abstract pattern from the messy drop of black ink. The abstraction took shape into the face of *Cataba* – Satan himself. In horror, Pyotr crumpled the parchment paper and tossed it onto the floor, where it landed beside the two other letters he had started to write to his old governess in Paris.

Parchment paper was expensive, and he was ashamed of what he had done. A boy of fourteen should be responsible and mature, not frightened by imaginary ghosts of ink. He would have to...

There was a knock on the door.

"Pyotr?" a familiar voice sang out.

It belonged to Vladimir Stepanovich, the dearest, kindest soul Pyotr had ever met. And, the only boy here at the School of Jurisprudence who understood that Mozart was not dead. The great composer lived in the opera house, inside the miraculous voices of the tenors and the sopranos who performed the *Don Giovanni* opera on Friday and Saturday nights.

"Il mio tesoro intanto," Vladimir sang loudly in his best Italian as he sprang open the door, hiding his face behind a black cape.

Pyotr's heart quickened. The music of the aria flooded over him, and he responded to Vladimir's impromptu performance, repeating the opening phrase in Russian. "To my beloved, oh hasten," Pyotr sang and then added, "to comfort, to comfort and console my sad heart."

Vladimir dropped his cape as Pyotr continued singing and rushed forward. The two boys hugged, held each other a moment, and then stepped apart – flushed and breathless.

"Are you ready, my dearest?" Vladimir asked.

The grin on his face was infectious and Pyotr kicked away the crumpled letters littering the floor, as if to vanquish them for trying to spoil this moment. He had nearly forgotten tonight was the night he and Vladimir would experience *Don Giovanni* again, for the third time this month.

"You know I am, dear.... dear, my Vladimir," Pyotr laughed, still singing the aria with his own words and repeating and extending each syllable, "dear, dear, my Vlad-i-mir!"

They both laughed and quickly made their way to the opera house. It was overflowing with patrons that night, but being so nimble, they found unclaimed seats near the front, although off to the far side of the theatre.

As the performance began with a thundering blast in D minor, the boys sat staring at the empty stage. The brutal force of the opening chords lingered over them a few moments, followed by a dramatic, almost deathly silence until the ominous chord was deliciously repeated.

Pyotr's spine tingled.

He could feel the presence of Mozart in the opera house, announcing his immortality to anyone who could listen with their whole heart. As the overture sweetened to an impetuous confirmation of life and love, Pyotr thought again about his dear mother, in Heaven now, surely.

Vladimir, sitting beside him turned and smiled. His face was not that of a boy, but of an angel radiating love in its most pure form. The two boys stared at each other. No words were needed. *Herr* Mozart's music took care of all they wished to say.

When finally, the performers took to the stage and the first aria began, Vladimir reached his slender hand across the seat and took hold of Pyotr's. The touch was warm and Pyotr responded by squeezing Vladimir's hand in return, lost in the magic of excited feelings coming from both the stage and the person beside him. *oh for crying out loud. ...*

It was only a few weeks later that the first true taste of winter arrived. This morning it bit into Pyotr's face. The wind and blowing snow nearly blinded him as he hurried toward school with Sergei and Vladimir.

The friends were as close as any three boys could be, so much so that Pyotr was often lost in his emotions towards them – and embarrassed by the impurity of his feelings.

"Hurry, you little frozen goats," Sergei laughed as he pushed Pyotr from behind. "I need time to lick you dry!"

Vladimir, the main trickster and constant singer in the group as well as the one never short for a quick retort, pushed Pyotr from the other side. "Lick you dry and eat your pie!"

Despite the vulgar words, Pyotr smiled and shook his head. Why did these songs – these crude little ditties – cause him such excitement? They awakened feelings no boy should feel, but still...

"Pyotr, Pyotr, Pyotr," Vladimir sang, "my dearest, dearest Pyotr, don't make it so *hard* for me... or I'll make it *hard* for you!"

Sergei screamed in delight and just as they reached the door of the school, almost an hour before the first class would begin, he jumped on Pyotr, pushing him into the snowbank and washing his face with snow.

But rather than be upset, Pyotr laid back in the snowbank and let Sergei wipe his face clean until the snow melted on his lips under the gentle, but persistent attention of his friend's long fingers.

"Stop it, you two *devushki!*" Vladimir sang. "Come! The door's open!"

───────

THE PIANOFORTE AT THE FRONT OF THE CLASSROOM WAS USED just about every day as part of instruction at the School of Jurisprudence. Whether it was to inspire, entertain or just provide a little relief when the professor himself was losing interest in the lesson, Pyotr did not know.

And he did not care.

He could use this instrument to say things that words alone could never express.

"Can we dance to your waltz?" Sergei asked as he and Vladimir stood waiting for Pyotr to begin.

"Of course," Pyotr replied. "But please, don't be silly. This is for her."

The two boys standing in front of him dropped their heads.

"We know," Vladimir said with a tone of respect. "You wrote it for Mama, your Mama. God bless her soul in Heaven."

"Thank you," Pyotr replied. "I only pray she might hear it and understand how much she is still in my heart."

He opened his music sheets and trembled a little as he placed his hands on the keys of the pianoforte. This would be so feeble he thought, compared to Mozart who he knew had already composed whole operas and symphonies by this age.

Nonetheless, Pyotr had decided without telling even his most beloved companions, the two boys standing right in front of him, he had decided he would devote his life to music, even though his tutor had told him there was no future as a 'musical' in Russia.

"Let us hear it!" Sergei pleaded. "We want to dance before another day of boredom starts."

Pyotr nodded and began to play. Slowly, he let the sound rise from the pianoforte, the hammers inside striking the strings with decided purpose. The classroom was filled with the music of the waltz and though it might not be as fine as the overture from *Don Giovanni,* it carried Sergei and Vladimir around the room a dozen times over.

As he watched them dancing to his music, a creation offered up to his mother in Paradise, Pyotr knew that whatever happened to his dreams, nothing would ever spoil the memory of this moment.

consistent crap!

CHAPTER 2

The ominous opening chords of Beethoven's 5th, the simple yet charming flute melody of Grieg's 'Morning Mood', or the overture of Rossini's *Wilhelm Tell;* we may not all be able to name the piece when we hear it, but we certainly recognize the melodies, in the same way famous words ring familiar as they are translated and repeated around the world.

Whether we realize it or not, classical music is still one of the most popular genres in existence, and we encounter it on a daily basis. It still features heavily in movies, video games, TV series, public events and commercials. All of us are familiar with at least a few works from that period of musical history.

A large portion of the music that is generally referred to as 'classical' stems from a time in musical history that is known as 'the common practice period', ranging from approximately 1600 to 1900 AD. It was a period of considerable evolution of the musical art, and many modern musical styles and genres have sprung from it.

In fact, thanks to their common roots and despite the obvious change in style, the differences between music from that era and the music we can now hear on popular radio are not as big as one might think. Many guidelines, principles, and best practices from the days of Bach, Haydn and Beethoven still go strong in today's chart toppers.

Of course, there were plenty of composers before this common practice period, and there is an enormous body of music dating back thousands of years from all over the world. It can be easy to forget that Western classical music is merely a part of a much larger whole, especially as it has become so widespread and well known.

Religion, and in particular Catholicism, played an important role in the growth and development of the Western musical tradition. However, there was ambiguity towards the role of music in worship, as it had associations with 'pagan' worship and could be considered seductive and distracting from the contemplation of God., Fortunately, it was generally agreed that music also fuelled devotion, and that its beauty reminded us of the glory of God.

written for 14-year olds ?

DEVELOPMENT OF COUNTERPOINT

THE CHRISTIAN MUSICAL REPERTOIRE GREW STEADILY OVER time, and gave birth to an important aspect of musical theory: counterpoint. Derived from the Latin *punctus contra punctum*, or 'point against point', counterpoint provides the rules and guidelines for the composition of melodic lines and their interaction. An important work in this field was written in 1725 by Johann Joseph Fux. His *Gradus ad Parnassum,* an extensive treatise on counterpoint and its various species, was studied intensively by composers for many centuries. One of these was Johann Sebastian Bach, whose works are considered the paramount examples of craftsmanship in counterpoint to this very day.

Over time, composers shifted focus from choral composition

to compositions for solo instruments, quartets and, later on, full size symphonic orchestras. As their musical compositions grew more complex, musical theory and practice evolved with them. Without the limitations of human vocal performers, new ideas arose, adding to the body of musical theory. The common practice period was the arena for these artistic battles, and there were certainly casualties; as the Ionian and Aeolian modes (more commonly known as the major and minor scales) emerged victorious, others retreated into the background. Conventions arose in the field of harmony (the relations between tonal combinations), and with the evolution of orchestral music, orchestration as a craft was born.

PYOTR IS BORN

By the time Pyotr Ilyich Tchaikovsky was born on 7 May 1840, the Western musical tradition had evolved into a rich and complex one, with pioneers and heroes such as Bach, Beethoven, Haydn, Handel and Mozart having left their everlasting mark on the cultural world. It's hardly surprising that young Pyotr and his friends were often exposed to and moved by their works.

During their rules, Peter the Great and Catherine I enacted many reforms in Russia aimed at modernizing the country, which generally entailed the import of Western ideas, styles and practices. These reforms, ranging broadly from music and art to industry and education, brought about a cultural divide in Russia.

The growth of Western influence in economic and cultural aspects of Russian society was often met with heavy resistance from those who did not wish to abandon their cultural heritage. As a welcome part of these reforms, there had been an import of Western music into the country; for instance, making it possible for young Pyotr to enjoy performances of Mozart's Don Giovanni.

When learning to play the piano in his childhood, he had already become acquainted with piano works from Western composers; such works would, at that time, be part of the 'fashionable repertoire', and certainly something a young student of the piano would learn to play. We know that young Pyotr was familiar with some of the work of Frederic Chopin, though he would not become a fan of the Polish composer's work, instead preferring the works of Robert Schumann.

Throughout his youth he was also exposed to vastly different sorts of music, such as Russian and Baltic folk songs and works created by traditional Russian composers, many of whom used a very different style than their Western counterparts. One of the most influential of these was Mikhail Ivanovich Glinka, whose work drew from folk tunes and was considered the epitome of Russian classical music. His works would serve as inspiration and guidance for a group of Russian composers whose stories intertwine with Tchaikovsky's; Pyotr, in more ways than one, would often find himself distanced (and even alienated) from his Russian contemporaries, and often in conflict with those who did not share his 'Western' tastes.

It would be these very tastes, however, that would ensure his legacy still lives on today. His works are performed all over the world, and the name Tchaikovsky is firmly established as one of the great masters in musical history.

CHAPTER 3

SAINT PETERSBURG, 1859 (AGE 19)

"I need you to deliver this," growled the bearded man hunched over the desk in front of Pyotr. The man dipped his steel pen in the inkwell, then signed a document with a monumental flourish that reminded Pyotr of an impassioned conductor urging his orchestra to begin.

"Sir, I am new here, and..." Pyotr hesitated.

He'd only been at the Ministry of Justice for a few days. A month ago he had celebrated his nineteenth birthday with more vodka and boisterous horseplay than he cared to admit. Now, completely sober in a stiffly pressed collar, he stared stupidly at the chief of the Accounting and Records Department. He was a boss who seemed to think everyone could see the thoughts dancing inside his head.

The chief raised his eyebrows. Had he already forgotten Pyotr was there?

"And *what,* young man?" the man snapped.

Pyotr froze, unable to produce a sound, to form any sort of question. The man shook his head, released a disgusted grunt, and carefully folded the signed document in half. He extended the sheaf of paper to Pyotr.

"This is a requisition, signed by me, establishing the Thirteenth of May, Eighteen Fifty-Nine, as the last date for receipt of all new encumbrances on departmental budgets in excess of the amounts already set forth in the preceding calendar year," the chief explained in a tone he likely reserved for those he considered somewhat below the standing of imbecile. With but four days' seniority as a civil servant, Pyotr assumed that was precisely how he was being viewed.

"Now that we are clear on *what*," the chief explained as Pyotr took the folded paper from him, "go straight upstairs, to the offices of the secretary of the Minister of Justice, and deliver this requisition. Be sure it is received, dated, and stamped, and return with a receipt of its delivery."

Pyotr had never been upstairs, let alone to the office of the Minister. Still, he was confident he could complete this simple assignment. He bowed his head, turned on his heel and left the chief's office.

He had worked hard to get this position, and harder still to quell the voice inside of him, or at least the voice of his father, his *Papasha,* who thought he might have a future as a musical artist. Everyone else, including Pyotr, thought this was surely a path to ruin.

"Pyotr!" someone hissed as he reached the end of the long hall that opened to a wide staircase. "Come and see this!"

He turned to the striking young man, Ivan, who had also recently started with the Ministry. He too was a clerk, assigned to menial roles, but since his father was an important official in the Ministry, Ivan had secured a small office and desk.

Pyotr was intrigued. "What is it?"

"I'll show you... in my office."

Inside the tiny space, Ivan lifted a cloth to uncover a canvas sitting on top of his desk. It was a finely detailed sketch of a naked woman. The woman's face seemed familiar.

"Is that..."

"Yes, it's Berta!"

Pyotr covered his mouth. "Berta Frideburg? The Minister's..." he gasped, "wife?"

"Yes! Indeed!" Ivan exclaimed. "She came to our house last week. I think I am truly in love with her!"

"Ivan, no, no," Pyotr responded gently. "But," he studied the artwork, "your technique is quite refined." He stood staring at the canvas, hopeful no one would burst into the office.

Ivan began to babble on about Berta, explaining how his heart beat faster when she came close to him, as she had last weekend at the dinner his father had arranged.

Pyotr listened, nodding his head for a while, then chided Ivan in a serious counsel about how he should handle his feelings, and hide this picture. As Pyotr talked, he tore off bits of the requisition he was holding and chewed it. His mind raced at what might happen if Ivan's secret and this drawing were discovered.

He tore off another bit of the signed requisition paper, chewed it and continued offering advice.

Ivan sobbed. "I can't live without knowing her, wrapping her in my arms as my truest love, as the man she must surrender her heart to and all that she is to me and..."

He suddenly looked up at Pyotr. "What is that document you are ripping up and chewing?"

Pyotr flinched. "Oh my!"

He looked down at the paper. He had torn away all the corners and chewed on it, a habit he'd developed with theatre tickets and programs. He held up the mutilated sheet of paper. "It's a signed requisition from my chief that I was taking to the Minister."

Ivan stopped sobbing. "You'll be dismissed!" He grabbed the paper from Pyotr. "Hurry! You need to recopy it, and get it signed again."

Pyotr stood stupidly as Ivan produced a clean sheet of white parchment, and began to copy out the requisition. The two said nothing as Ivan neatly reproduced the document and then handed it back to Pyotr.

"Take this and pray your chief forgives you," he whispered, his eyes wide and serious, "or your career as a civil servant may be a very short one indeed."

Two years later, 1861... (Age 21)

Lent was the worst of times.

It meant all the things Pyotr despised most about Petersburg. It was forty days of stinking butter rotting in the larder. Lean fish as appetizing as river water. Lenten vespers preceded by masses followed by more masses, foul roads and Tsar Alexander's boring *tableaux vivants*. Living portraits of Russia's glory?

No. More like subjugated men and women posing stiffly in silent stupidity, their passions drained from a lack of meat, cheese and tobacco.

But thankfully, Lent was still a few days away and he was finding this year's *maslenitsa*, the annual shrovetide celebrations or 'pancake week' as everyone called it, the best Pyotr could ever remember. Vodka and cigarettes. Vodka and blinis. Vodka and cheese and most importantly, vodka and...

"Victor!" Pyotr shouted as he waited in the square for a bubbling blini to finish frying on the open stove. The old lady cooking the pancake rarely smiled, but her little circles of crêpe deliciousness, cut in the shape of the sun, lit up the face of everyone lucky enough to buy one from her.

She flipped the golden blini and slid it onto Pyotr's waiting plate. He pursed his lips toward her, offering a kiss. He was rewarded with a toothy grin and he couldn't resist leaning closer and smooching her hairy chin.

"Bah," she grunted. *"Ukhodi!"* She shooed him away, shaking her head with a smile.

He laughed, covering the steaming blini with gooseberry jam, sour cream and honey. Victor came running toward him, breathless and excited.

"The *troika* race... it's almost time!" he exclaimed, his face wet from the soft snowflakes starting to fall again.

"I know, I know," Pyotr smiled. He cut a chunk of the blini dripping in jam and honey and offered it to Victor.

"Mmmmm... heavenly." Victor smiled as Pyotr fed his new friend, a young cavalry-grenadier lieutenant from the Hussars of the Imperial Guard.

They had met just last week at one of the clubs for men that preferred the company of other men. Pyotr's fingers wiped away some of the sticky honey that dribbled from Victor's lips, feeling a jolt of excitement from the discreet intimacy.

Victor finished the rest of the blini in a few gulps. He reached for his wineskin, filled with vodka and washed down the pancake before offering Pyotr a sip. The tip was still wet from Victor's lips as he squeezed a shot of liquor into Pyotr's mouth.

"Come on!" Victor cried after pumping another shot into his own mouth. "Let's get a good spot to see the race!"

He grabbed Pyotr's hand and the two fought their way through the market square, filled with singing and dancing men, women and children. Fat snowflakes were falling from the sky in a cloud of airy whiteness. No one seemed to mind as the music from a group of musicians raised their tempo and volume. A man on accordion was playing a lively song, accompanied by another keeping time on three wooden spoons.

As they fought for a spot near where the horse-drawn sleds were set to start the *troika* race, the bright colours of the women's scarves and shawls caught Pyotr's eye. Together with the softly falling snowflakes, the vodka warming him still and the infectious music of the accordion, spoons and *balalaika* guitar gathering momentum, he wished this moment with Victor might never end.

Victor touched his shoulder. "You like the music, Pyotr?"

"Indeed!"

Without another word, Victor pushed away some of the people crowding against them, jumped in the air and landed in a crouched position, arms outstretched. With two loud claps he began to dance, a *hopak* style of high leaps, squatting kicks and turns that Pyotr had long admired. The men and women around started clapping and soon Victor was performing with an exuberance and a twinkling of the eye that made Pyotr's heart melt.

Later, back in Victor's flat, the perfect afternoon was easing into an idyllic evening. As they sat together, smoking cigarettes and rubbing shoulders, Victor questioned Pyotr about his dreams.

"It's not important," he replied after taking a long thoughtful drag from his cigarette. "But I have often considered music as a career. My *papasha* thinks maybe I still can, but..." He let the words float through the smoky flat, lingering and then evaporating like his own self-doubt.

"But what?" Victor asked gently, rubbing Pyotr's leg.

"To be a musical in Russia is to suffer, to know only a broken heart, a broken spirit," Pyotr replied, his eyes growing wet. "Much better to devote myself with greater seriousness to being the best civil servant lawyer I can be."

Victor stood up and removed his sweater. His bare chest rippled like a beacon of strength, promising the kind of fulfillment Pyotr longed to experience.

"Your eyes betray you, *kotik*," Victor whispered. "Passion comes from truth."

He placed his hands on his hips, toying with the belt that held his trousers in place. "And you must set free the truth of who you are... and all that you are meant to be."

THE NEXT MORNING PYOTR LAY STILL BESIDE VICTOR, listening to the rhythmic nature of his deep and steady breathing. It was a soothing tone, a steady and strong cadence that brought a feeling of hope somehow.

They were both naked under the blanket.

Though he should feel only guilt for the unnatural sins they consummated last night, Pyotr couldn't find it within him to harbour such negative feelings. There was a raw desire and tender compassion – and if that was a sin in the eyes of the Tsar and the Church, so be it.

His mind wandered to the startling revelation after they had spent their passion and lay still beside each other. Victor had attended musical-theory classes set up for dilettantes by none other than the composer Nikolay Zaremba. Victor had learned enough about counterpoint to make Pyotr laugh with his impression of how the stern and strict Nikolay had taught it.

And most intriguing of all was the sheet music Victor shared with Pyotr. It was a piano theme and though he was too tired last night to study it closely, it now played in Pyotr's head and tugged at his fingers.

Quietly, he slipped out of bed, grabbed the sheet music from the bedside table, and quickly donned a robe and slippers. He padded over to the adjoining parlour, sat down at Victor's piano and opened the sheet music. It wasn't anything so grand as a Beethoven symphony, but compelling in its own simple counterpoint structure. It echoed the tradition of Bach as only the old master could do with such adherence to form.

His fingers touched the keys. The first few bars were nothing, but after he ran through the entire piece once, he realized how powerful the overall effect could be. He played it again, the notes already fixed in his head. He no longer required the sheet music.

The third time Pyotr let his fingers make their own decisions. They danced away from the strict counterpoint technique, tickling and teasing out new variations. He laughed to himself as he turned the whole structure upside down and began to stretch it more and more. He was lost in his improvisations when suddenly a strong hand touched his shoulder and a warm whisper caressed his ear.

"You fly with angels," the voice spoke.

Pyotr stopped playing and turned to Victor, his face only inches away. "Angels?"

"Yes, they carry you with them. You have no choice but to follow where they lead."

Pyotr hung his head. His father had encouraged him to choose a musical path, but he still couldn't believe it was possible. "I'm scared, Victor. I want more than anything to write music, a symphony like..." he hesitated, afraid to even speak the name.

"Beethoven?"

Pyotr bit his lip. He wanted to feel pain, to hurt himself. "Yes, but I am woefully lacking in the technique of composition. I do not even know how much..." he hesitated, "how much I do not know."

Victor sat down beside him on the piano bench. Pyotr's hands rested on the keys. Victor laid his own hands over them and pushed down. The hammers of the piano knocked against the strings in a plaintive cacophony.

"You, my friend, are a musician from tip to toe," Victor said, mixing his commanding authority with a passionate inflection. "Listen to me."

With one hand he gripped Pyotr's face gently, turning it toward him. "Above everything else you must apply yourself to music. You must be serious. You must study and learn. I will not fail to encourage and support you, even when you give up on yourself."

Pyotr felt himself trembling. He could not hold back his tears a second longer. As they washed over his face and Victor touched his wet lips to his, Pyotr knew his dream might have a chance.

A FEW MONTHS LATER...

Without so much as a word, the hulking figure strode across the front of the ornately furnished classroom. His black mane, only partially tamed with thick wax, framed his stout face, broad nose and dark eyes.

Pyotr couldn't help but shrink a little in the presence of Anton Rubinstein, the man the other students referred to as 'Master'. He was not just a pianist, a composer and a conductor. He was a brute force of nature exploding into the windowless chamber deep inside Mikhailovsky Palace where Pyotr had been lucky enough to get a spot for today's demonstration on musical composition.

Now that he was twenty-one years old and had a steady job at the Ministry, this session at the new Russian Musical Society was something he was attending only to please Victor and perhaps *Papasha*. Still, Pyotr was glad they pushed him so hard. Otherwise, he would still be in bed this morning – lazy, drunk and full of guilt.

Anton Rubinstein sat down heavily on the bench in front of the polished black piano that dominated the room. He placed his hands on the keys. His thick fingers, each the size of a kielbasa sausage, seemed almost grotesque next to the narrow strips of ivory and ebony that fronted the magnificent instrument.

He breathed deeply for a moment or two, as if gathering air for a journey beneath the sea.

And then with a powerful perfection that Pyotr had never before seen, the teacher began. The first few tonic chords of Beethoven's piano sonata *Appassionata,* Opus 57 gave way to delicate fluttering, like crystal-winged doves hovering in the air. As he let them slowly descend, his hands reached across to the lowest notes of the five octaves available to him and somehow managed to gallop up the keyboard with his meaty fingers coaxing out a trill, repeating the entire phrase a half-tone higher.

Pyotr had practiced this same sonata many times, but never had it sounded anything like this. His mouth gaped open as the trill ended with a short dark phrase from the angry bowels of the piano followed by sharp alternating chords and half-tone fragments. His teacher was lost in the fury of his performance, throwing his lion-like head back as if in triumph of the beast he had slain.

And then Anton Rubinstein stopped, hung his head a second and turned to the ten young men who sat staring at him. Pyotr had never witnessed raw talent like this, an artist who played with the power of Jupiter and yet at the same time teased the heart like a yearling fawn in the mist.

"Man is a fickle and disreputable creature," the teacher finally spoke, rising from the piano bench. Anton's stocky face and sweaty hands belied the talent he had just demonstrated. He fixed Pyotr in his gaze. "Do you know who wrote those words?"

Pyotr flushed. He did not. It seemed all his foolish pleasures and vices had dulled him into not knowing much of anything anymore. "No, sir," he replied weakly. "I'm ashamed to say I have no idea."

"Your shame is well deserved!" Anton bellowed. "It flowed from the pen of Fyodor Dostoyevsky, your own countryman." He glared at the other students in the class. "Can *anyone* finish this passage?"

It seemed no one dared incur the teacher's wrath with a wrong answer.

Anton snorted. "Try to fix in your head a melody that might bring Dostoyevsky's words to the ear." He sat back down on the piano bench. "Man is a fickle and disreputable creature, and perhaps like a chess-player, is interested in the process of attaining his goal rather than the goal itself."

Pyotr made a note in his diary: 'Dostoyevsky... author.'

Anton sat back on the piano bench. "You are all here to learn the art of composition?" he asked, staring at the keys of the piano. "Do you know who wrote the music I played?"

This was something Pyotr did know. "Beethoven!" he proclaimed proudly.

Anton repeated the dark three-note sequence from the Opus 57 then fixed Pyotr with a stern look. "You are an admirer?"

"Of course! I wish to study his music to learn..."

"No!" Anton replied sharply. He rose from the piano bench and stood towering over Pyotr. "Listen to me. Listen, all of you. Or do not bother wasting my time."

The room was silent. Pyotr felt the hairs on his neck standing at attention like frightened soldiers ready to hoist the white flag.

Anton scowled. "You must not *study* Beethoven's music."

All the eyes were upon him. "His music must be *reincarnated.* Reincarnated by you." He looked away, staring down at the piano keys.

"That is your only goal."

THE WORDS RUNG IN PYOTR'S EARS AFTER THE SHORT CLASS was over. He sat frozen in his chair, all alone in the empty chamber.

"Reincarnated by you."

How does one do that? How do you reincarnate Beethoven?

Pyotr had ability, perhaps even a gift. But this was asking too much. He told his sister Sasha that he was a 'dandy' – dancing and frolicking about Petersburg, playing giddy piano quartets for amusement, merrily visiting friends and trying desperately to understand the darkness that blanketed him most days.

It was a cloak he hid beneath, hidden from almost everyone.

"I have an illness," he explained to her. "I call it, 'Oblomovism.' I am lazy. I spend more rubles than I earn. My finances are desperate, yet I do nothing to remedy the situation and stupidly hope not to end up in the debtors' prison. I am truly more slothful than Oblomov himself, who could barely leave his bed to pee."

The main character from Ivan Goncharov's novel struck a

chord with Pyotr. Being like Oblomov was his greatest fear, but a fate he seemed drawn toward following, he wrote to Sasha. "If I fail to vanquish it, I could very easily go under. But fortunately, there is still some time left."

Though his sister no doubt read his letter with concern, only Victor – dear sweet Victor – seemed to truly understand Pyotr's self-doubt.

A shadow darkened the room. "Well, *kotik?*"

It was Victor, smartly dressed in the crisply tailored uniform of the Russian Imperial Guard. Pyotr struggled to reply. "Anton Rubinstein gave me more than I could have hoped to find in one lesson, but..."

Victor touched the back of Pyotr's neck, massaging the top of his spine. Memories of their nights together flooded over him.

"Your fear is holding you back," Victor said softly. "It is not who you are... we both know what lies within you, dormant... undiscovered."

He lifted his hand from Pyotr's neck. The loss of pleasure was jarring.

"Come with me," Victor said, turning in a precise military manoeuvre. His leather boots slid across the marble floor, as he snapped his heels together and marched out the door.

Pyotr followed and shortly afterwards sat on a chair across from one of the most distinguished looking men he had ever met. His neatly trimmed beard, and jet-black hair framed a face with piercing eyes that were both inquisitive and sympathetic.

Victor sat in a chair beside Pyotr. "Nikolay Ivanovich... Zaremba," he began his introductions, "I am pleased to present Pyotr Ilyich Tchaikovsky."

"Nikolay Ivanovich," Pyotr repeated. "It is a great honour to finally meet you."

This provoked a chuckle from Nikolay. "From what Victor has told me, it is I who should be honoured."

Pyotr flushed. "Thank you, but I have more desire than talent."

Nikolay Zaremba stared back. Whatever he might be thinking, his face conveyed only warmth. "Victor believes you would benefit," he paused, "or should I say, you may find *inspiration,* in learning the principles of music theory – the rules of harmony, the structure of composition."

"I would indeed," Pyotr replied. Though he thirsted to compose, building a house that would last generations started with a mastery of construction techniques.

"May I ask you, which opera do you most prefer? Glinka's *A Life for the Tsar,* or ..."

"No, no. *Don Giovanni,* by far!" Pyotr interrupted, then cowered in his chair, thinking that perhaps preference for an Austrian over the father of Russian music was not a good way to introduce himself.

The bearded teacher smiled. He leaned closer to Pyotr. "I think we may get along very well, but one more request, please, if you are to become my student. Would you play for me?" He pointed to the piano at the back of the room.

Victor turned in his chair and caught Pyotr's eye with a discreet nod. Pyotr hadn't prepared for this. He slowly rose from his chair, and made his way hesitantly to the piano and sat down.

"What would you like to hear?" he asked, turning toward Nikolay Zaremba.

"Something that speaks to your spirit, to the music inside of you," Nikolay replied.

Pyotr sat thinking a moment. Mozart was a 'musical Christ,' but Beethoven... well, he was like God in the Old Testament – fire and brimstone, power and sadness, deeply aware of the tragedy of being human.

Pyotr's fingers touched the keys. Without knowing why, he began to play Beethoven's 'Andante favori in F major.' He knew it was a composition the composer often performed as it was so well loved by his audiences. It was stunningly simple – sparse and compact, modulating from F to D flat major and then back again.

Almost nine minutes later he came to the end of the rondo, lost completely by the music. Though he had no sheet music to guide him, Pyotr could see the whole score in his head.

The room was quiet, but his heart thumped wildly. He had nothing left inside, having poured out all he loved and ever wanted to be through the keys of this marvellous piano.

Nikolay rose from his chair and approached him. "Your friend was correct, Pyotr Ilyich."

He looked up at the teacher.

"You are not a government clerk," Nikolay said with a tone that gladdened Pyotr. "You performed the work of the composer I most admire. And using perfect technique and in a manner that seems to come straight from your heart."

"Thank you, Nikolay Ivanovich." Pyotr bowed his head.

"No, thank you, Pyotr Ilyich," the teacher replied. "If you will have me as your teacher, the honour will truly be mine."

AS THEY LEFT THE MIKHAILOVSKY PALACE BEHIND, SHUFFLING through the frigid air and light snow of a Petersburg's autumn evening, Pyotr and Victor remained silent until the palace was far off in the distance.

Victor, walking ahead, stopped and turned around. "Now, do you understand?"

Though he knew what Victor implied, Pyotr was not ready to believe. "I understand only that I have much to learn from these men, and yes I will study with them, but..."

"But what?" Victor's face was tight, his eyebrows raised.

"I have debts, many debts, and if I can secure a promotion at the Ministry, even another twenty rubles a month, I can extinguish them..."

"No!" Victor interrupted. "You must quit your position, forget the Ministry. You are not a clerk. Your path lies there."

He pointed to the misty outline of the palace, softened in the dim light and by swirling flakes of snow. "The men there, Anton Grigoryevich and Nikolay Ivanovich, *they* are your future. Why can you not see what they so clearly observe and offer?"

"But my debts, I can't..."

"Your debts are to yourself, *kotik*." Victor interjected, his tone softening. "And now, you must decide by yourself." He paused a moment, brushing melting snow from his face. "I'm not sure you will see me again for a long time."

Pyotr winced. "What?" He felt a shiver of fear. "Why?"

"The serfs have been freed by the emperor, and now that they are emancipated the world has changed. I have been transferred to Moscow to prepare for a new assignment, somewhere in the eastern empire."

Snowflakes gathered on both of them as they stood in silence, their faces wet and cold. "I can't do this without you," Pyotr rasped.

"You can. And you will," Victor replied, wiping Pyotr's cheeks. "Someday when you have made your name, give me whatever credit you think worthy. And know I will carry you in my heart... forever."

Five years later, 1866
Countryside near Saint Petersburg (Age 26)

"I HATE MANKIND IN THE MASS," PYOTR SCREECHED AT THE dour physician who sat cold as granite at the foot of the bed. The light from a single candle cast the doctor's shadow like a demon of the dead across the wall behind Pyotr.

"Hate?" the doctor growled like the devil himself.

"Yes! I want to go to a place without people."

The doctor rose from the chair. Pyotr could not understand how this devil physician had come to this tiny cottage far from

the city, in the dead of night. The doctor bent over him and
pulled the skin down from beneath Pyotr's left eye, holding the
candle up higher, moving it closer.

"When did you last sleep?" the doctor asked, peering in
closer and closer.

Pyotr tried to recall. The days and nights blurred together
and even now he wasn't sure if he was hallucinating. Demons and
angels had come calling, Germans and Russians too, men and
women, brothers and sisters, friends and...

"Do you know where you are?" the monster doctor asked,
prodding with his other finger now, stretching Pyotr's right eye
open.

"I'm not afraid of you, Lucifer. I don't have long to live, but
you cannot steal my music - I keep it locked in here." He
touched his head. "Even you have no power to steal it from me...
to chastise it."

The dark figure, half man-half devil, groped for Pyotr's wrist.
He held it a moment and in that few seconds anger swelled deep
within Pyotr, until sensing the end of his mortality at hand he
cried out in fear. "Forgive all that I am," he sobbed. "Have mercy
on my soul."

"Pyotr Ilyich," the man spoke. "You are going mad and unless
you find a way to exorcise this darkness, you will not escape the
fate that now calls for you."

———

THE NEXT MORNING PYOTR WOKE BRIEFLY.

It was well past ten o'clock. He should be up taking tea,
preparing to give a lesson that would bring in a few more rubles
against his mounting debt. He should be slaving over his
symphony, the first composition that was truly his and his
alone.

Instead, he closed his eyes and let sleep take hold once again.
He vaguely remembered the bitter potion on his lips from the

demon who had called upon him last night. The potion's work it seemed was not yet complete.

Ten hours later he managed to lift himself up, pull on his smock and boil water for tea.

Alone in the little cottage secured for him by his sister and his father, he sat staring at his composition – his first completely independent symphony, since graduating from the Conservatoire in Petersburg.

The first movement, *Daydreams of a Winter Journey, Allegro tranquillo* in G minor, was seven hundred and twenty-three bars of soul-crushing despair.

"Winter Daydreams?" he hissed.

Even the subtitle for his symphony was inappropriate, according to both Anton Rubinstein and Nikolay Zaremba. If it was only the title that troubled them, it would not be such a problem. However, they reserved their most intense displeasure for the work itself.

"We would never allow this to be performed by our orchestra," Nikolay told him. "You follow neither convention nor protocol of everything I taught you the last five years."

Anton was even harsher. "There is no evidence of the promise you displayed during your time with us. You are neither German nor Russian, and you please neither. If you do not change your approach, we will not waste our time on such music as this."

The words were biting from the two teachers who had most inspired him. They clung to European tradition as ferociously as the 'five' rebellious Russian composers rejected it. Anton was right about one thing though; both camps despised Pyotr's work and unless he grovelled before Rubinstein and Zaremba, his work would never be heard by anyone.

He poured some vodka into a glass and set it down beside his steaming tea. His life was not worth much. His debts continued to mount. His lovers were fewer and further apart. Only his family – his father, sisters and brothers seemed to care if he lived or died.

Pyotr's first symphony might well be his last. He raised the glass of vodka to his lips and began to cry. Tears ran down his cheeks, spilling over his lips until they mingled with the liquor.

"No!" he shouted. "No! No!"

He smashed the glass against the stone wall of the cottage and threw his hand down on the table. The papers of his symphony flew up and he batted them away in disgust. They fell onto the floor and he fell on top of them, longing to feel the music caress his spirit, like all the loves he had ever found.

They were gone now and if he was not to descend completely into madness, he would need to find a way to remain among the living.

CHAPTER 4

"You are neither German nor Russian, and you please neither."

This simple sentence and the judgement hidden therein sums up the long-lasting conflict Tchaikovsky would have with his musical contemporaries in Russia; not belonging to one or the other. It may be hard to imagine why this remark by Zaremba would be so troubling to young Pyotr Ilyich Tchaikovsky during work on his first symphony. Why not simply shrug it off and follow his own tastes and path? Why not let ring clearly the unique voice that the world would come to admire as his own?

To understand the implication of this remark and the creative disagreement between Tchaikovsky and his fellow Russian composers, we must first examine what it means for his music to sound neither German nor Russian. To do that, we must understand the underlying principles of musical composition: counterpoint and harmony.

Counterpoint is a compositional technique that deals with the writing of multiple melodic lines. These lines have a harmonic relationship to each other but are otherwise independent with regard to rhythm and melodic shape.

Let's break that down for a moment.

The first part of the definition seems straightforward enough; writing multiple melodic lines. Anyone with access to a musical instrument (including the human voice) can do so rather quickly. All one has to do is to record two different melodies, even as simple as singing the first notes of a scale such as 'do re mi fa sol', the so called 'fixed do' system where 'do' indicates the note C.

A melody is, in essence, nothing more than a sequence of notes. Whether the melody is pleasing, original or complex, is irrelevant to the definition; any sequence of notes can be considered a melody. Even just hitting random single keys in sequence on a piano produces a melody. To satisfy the criterion of 'multiple melodic lines', one merely has to repeat the process with different notes to create a second melody.

If we were to then play these melodies together, chances are it will sound dreadful. This should not be surprising, as we didn't write the second melody in relation to the first one; we did not consider how these lines would interact with each other. This brings us to the next part of the definition: the harmonic relationship between the two melodies. But what constitutes a 'harmonic relationship'?

Harmony in music describes, in the simplest sense, the simultaneous sounding of two or more notes. Two notes sounding together can either be dissonant or consonant; as the names suggest, the former describes two notes sounding tensed, yearning for resolution, even jarring. The easiest way to hear such dissonance is by pressing two white keys next to each other on the piano at the same time. The effect is not a particularly pleasing sound by itself, creating a sense of tension.

Dissonant sounding notes yearn to resolve into a more pleasing and restful combination, which is what the consonant sounding notes bring to the table. This effect of tension versus relaxation, restless versus calm, is crucial to musical composition: it is the art of combining such effects that breathes life into a musical piece. A composition using merely dissonants is not pleasing to listen to, as it brings no points of calm or repose. In the same way, however, a piece with only consonants will sound boring and predictable; the lack of tension takes away the effect of coming to a resting point, as the entire piece now exists of only restful tones.

Counterpoint provides rules and guidelines on how to employ consonants and dissonants in the interaction between the melodic lines being crafted. Though it may seem odd to encounter a term such as 'rules' when talking about art, this is how they are referred in many works on the subject. It can help to consider these rules as the distilled wisdom and experience of composers of the past. Following these rules during the compositional process ensures that the result will sound good, though not necessarily original, or amazing.

The final part of our definition of counterpoint refers to independence, which may need some clarification:

Consider once more two melodic lines. They consist of the same notes, with the same duration. One line, however, moves upwards through the notes, and the other downwards. Though they are undoubtedly not the same melody, they're also not very independent of each other; one could be considered merely an inversion of the other. True independence between melodic lines in counterpoint means a distinct difference between the curve of the melody and the rhythm in the melodic lines.

Summarizing counterpoint in such a brief way could give the impression that it is a simple matter, and even though the rules and guidelines that counterpoint puts forth are indeed relatively simple, the complexity lies in their application. Counterpoint is often taught in 'species', which can be considered as difficulty levels. The first species of counterpoint introduces only part of the full set of rules and guidelines, dealing with note against note (which should remind us of the origin of the word 'counterpoint', or *punctus contra punctum* – point against point.

However, one might be hard pressed to find many musical

pieces that are thus written, apart from exercises for counter-point students.

As one progresses through the species of counterpoint, many more rules and guidelines are introduced, and the complexity of the melodic lines increases swiftly. Very soon, more than two melodic lines are brought into the equation, adding enormously to the complexity of the practical application of counterpoint. It takes mastery of the concept to create truly amazing works of music incorporating multiple melodic lines. The works of Johann Sebastian Bach, in particular his fugues and canons, are considered to be absolute highlights in the practical application of counterpoint.

Another principle of musical composition that was already briefly touched upon is that of harmony, two or more notes sounding together at the same time. Harmony describes the rules and guidelines of multiple notes sounding together, such as which notes are allowed to be in the bass (or lowest voice) in such a block of notes, which notes can be doubled and which cannot, and other considerations. It also describes the relation of one block of notes between its predecessor and/or successor, how the notes can move between these blocks, what the functions of these blocks are in the framework of the musical piece itself, and many more. It is also not hard to see the interaction between counterpoint and harmony, as choices in one can affect the possibilities in the other. Together, they become valuable tools to the composer to create a work of art that will be pleasing to the ear, employing the distilled wisdom and experience of past composers.

Thus, we come back to Zaremba's remark to young Pyotr and the underlying cause of Tchaikovsky's long-lasting creative disagreement with some of his Russian contemporaries.

The theories of harmony and counterpoint in the Western classical tradition evolved over time. A clear example of this is the distinction between 'strict' and 'free' counterpoint; the former being the traditional theory as it was taught from works such as 'Gradus ad Parnassum' by Johann Joseph Fux (1725), the latter being a form that does not observe the theoretical rules and guidelines as strictly, allowing for greater freedom in the compositional process.

Constructions that would have been absolutely forbidden in strict counterpoint, became allowed in free counterpoint. Reasons for these are plentiful, including the evolution of the orchestra to its present-day form, changing tastes of both the public and composers alike, and changes to the function of music as it became stronger as a separate artform and less subservient to religious purposes.

EVOLUTION OF HARMONY AND COUNTERPOINT

To illustrate how such a change could come about and what impact this would have had on existing theoretical frameworks, consider a church gathering taking place centuries ago, for example 1588, the time of Giovanni Pierluigi da Palestrina, a famous composer of sacred music.

The amassed worshippers would sing psalms and hymns during the gathering to praise God, and the function of music was one of support. Such 'sacred music' would be rather simple and, when considered from a theoretical musical perspective, somewhat unsurprising. One reason for this was that the music was not intended to divert attention from the worship itself, but to serve as an instrument in this worship. Another, much more practical reason was that those attending the worship were hardly trained singers; the music had to be simple enough for the everyday worshipper to sing along to.

This placed quite a few restraints on the creative freedom of a composer in this genre, and it's not surprising that many considerations in counterpoint regarding the construction of a melodic line had to do with its singability. The style of writing that this produced (and the works of Palestrina in particular) was the foundation of 'Gradus ad Parnassum', and several of the guidelines therein were derived directly from what was called 'the Palestrina style'. Johann Sebastian Bach and many other famous composers throughout studied the works of Palestrina meticulously.

With the birth of the orchestra, the dwindling of old modes in favour of the major and minor scales, and with composers seeking new and innovative paths of composing, harmony and counterpoint evolved as well. Some of the restrictions of strict counterpoint were let go, and the theory of harmony grew as the orchestra allowed for many different voices (or instruments) playing at the same time.

Orchestration as an aspect of the compositional process became much more prominent, educating students of composition in the art of working with such a large collection of varying instruments, all of them bringing a unique sound to the whole. This evolution never came to a stop; music styles evolve all the time, and one can experience this evolution first-hand by listening to modern popular music and comparing it to popular music from, say, the '60s.

There is one important influence that has not yet been touched upon, and that is the influence of geography, or more precisely perhaps, that of culture. We need only visit countries outside the region of Western culture to observe these influences. In architecture, we could note the differences between buildings in Japan and France from 200 years ago, especially in places of worship. In the visual arts, there is a notable difference between paintings from the Netherlands and those originating from the Baltic area.

These differences exist in music as well, influenced by the culture of the region. In Russia, where Pyotr Ilyich Tchaikovsky lived, there was a musical style quite different from that in Germany, France, or Italy. Here too, religion had played an important part in the formation of that style, as had folksongs and other secular music. Russian music had as much its own identity as did Western music of that time, and it is here that the hurt in Zaremba's remark lies:

"You are neither German nor Russian, and you please neither."

Tchaikovsky's style did not clearly belong to either the Russian or German musical identity (the latter being associated with composers such as Bach and Beethoven), and was, according to Tchaikovsky's mentor, unpleasant to both.

While the first part of this remark could be considered accurate, time would show that the second part of it was most certainly not.

CHAPTER 5

Heavy and insistent pounding shook the chamber door. "Pyotr!" The shrill voice of Nikolay Rubinstein cried as he rattled the handle. "We need to go... now!"

Pyotr closed his eyes. Nothing could stop the concert.

It would begin at precisely eight o'clock this evening, with or without him, in the plush splendour of the Imperial Bolshoi Petrovsky Theatre. His symphony in G Minor, his first and likely his last symphony, would finally be presented to Moscow's perfumed ladies and distinguished gentlemen.

"Go away," Pyotr whined. "I'm sick."

His stomach churned as he fought to keep the vodka and bread in his gut from rising to his throat again. He tore at his beard, flecked with chunks of spittle, and cried out in anguish as he tried to pull the hair from his face. The more pain he inflicted on himself the better.

"Come now!" Nikolay shouted. "This is your night!"

Pyotr felt the vomit rising as his stomach retched, emptying the stinking bile into a bucket. The putrid odour stung his nose. "Everyone will soon know," he wailed.

The pounding at the door grew louder. He dragged himself off the bed, stumbled forward and opened the door.

Nicholas stood before him, dressed in a crisp, white starched shirt, black jacket and top hat. "Soon know what?"

Pyotr held his mouth. "That I am not worth the price of their ticket."

Nikolay did not respond immediately. He held a paper book-let. Behind him the light of a dozen burning candles blazed. His eyes searched Pyotr's. "The words of my brother Anton," he said softly, "they haunt you still?"

Pyotr nodded. The stinging rebuke of the older Rubinstein brother lingered. *We will not waste our time on such music as this.'* The words hung like lead anvils over his spirit.

"Do you know why I invited you to live with me, Pyotr Ilyich?" Nikolay asked, studying the cover sheet of the symphony he would soon conduct, "and offered you a job teaching at the conservatory?"

"Abject pity?"

"*Nyet!*" Nikolay replied. "I knew only *you* could birth some-thing like this!" He held up the cover sheet titled in an ornate script: 'Daydreams of a Winter Journey, Symphony in G Minor by Pyotr Ilyich Tchaikovsky.'

"But it's not even been approved by – "

"By fools!" Nikolay's face grew red. "Only an audience can pronounce judgement. Ignore the rest!"

The two men stood silent a moment. A clock at the end of the hall kept time, measuring the beats.

Tick-tock.

Tick-tock.

Tick-tock.

"After two years, the hour approaches," Nikolay whispered. "It matters not what I or my brother or anyone else thinks."

He reached inside his jacket and handed Pyotr two tickets for tonight's performance at the Bolshoi. He tapped the tickets with his index finger.

"Very soon you will learn what *they* think."

THE LIGHT FROM A HUNDRED GOLD-TRIMMED CANDELABRA glittered between the rich crimson velvet draping of the private boxes that ringed all five levels of the towering Imperial Bolshoi Petrovsky Theatre.

Pyotr sank lower in his seat in the front row.

This great hall with its lavish gilt interior was almost full, and more people kept coming in and taking their seats. Each level greeted them with a different stucco arabesque. Beneath the gargantuan chandelier that hung hundreds of feet above him, Pyotr glanced around the hall in terror at the sea of faces – almost two thousand men and women, each a patron with high expectations, now murmuring and laughing, waiting to render judgement.

He couldn't help but raise his eyes to the blazing crystal chandelier high above his head, the light from each of its three hundred oil lamps burning to create a small sun over this cathedral to music and art.

On stage, the musicians carefully tuned their instruments. His score called for two flutes, two oboes, two clarinets, and two bassoons; wind instruments so crucial to invoke swirly snow and December bird song in his first movement. For darkness and depth there were four horns, two trumpets, three trombones, a tuba, two timpani, cymbals and bass drums. Finally and just as important, the strings; violins – one and two, along with the violas, cellos and double basses.

In front of each one of these accomplished musicians the notes of his music sat waiting impatiently to expose him to the world as a fraud.

Pyotr could hear each quaver of his heart. He could scarcely find breath to fill his lungs as he shivered in fits of anxious despair. Suddenly, Nikolay bounded across the stage and the murmuring of the audience ebbed.

A hand touched his shoulder from behind. A gentle voice

spoke in a hushed tone. "Master," a young man whispered with a warming breath upon Pyotr's neck. "I am so excited for you."

He turned around to confirm the speaker, Vladimir Shilovsky. He was the young prodigy in Pyotr's composition class at the Moscow Conservatory where Pyotr had worked these past two years, thanks to Nikolay's generosity.

"Thank you, Vladimir. I hope it pleases you."

Young Vladimir, a teenage boy with hopeful eyes and the face of a child, smiled – an angel sent from Heaven. "Everything you do pleases me," the lanky cherub whispered. "I came for the rehearsal and fell in love with every note that flowed from your pen."

Pyotr's eyes welled with grateful tears. "Thank you again, Vladimir, I hope I deserve such kind –"

His words were cut short by the first notes of music from the stage – transcendent strings hushing the glittering hall, inviting every ear into the 'Daydream of a Winter Journey.' As the tempo increased and the full majesty of the orchestra erupted, Pyotr felt the hand of young Vladimir on his back slowly release.

For the next forty-one minutes, Nikolay conducted the orchestra through the four movements of the symphony; *Allegro, Andante, Scherzo* and *Finale*. Pyotr cursed each tiny miscue, every awkward bar that didn't work as he'd hoped, every transition that failed to find its connection and each chord that wasn't quite right yet.

Then, thankfully, it was over. He sat fixed to his seat, awaiting the verdict of the court. And then, gloriously, a sound he had never imagined rose up around him.

Applause. Loud, vigorous, thundering applause!

He turned to see young Vladimir clapping wildly, his eyes overflowing, his hand raised up towards Pyotr in benevolent exaltation. Behind him a sea of smiling, clapping patrons stood cheering even more loudly.

"Ladies and gentlemen!" Nikolay boomed from the stage. "I give you Pyotr... Ilyich... Tchaikovsky and his first symphony!"

Vladimir leaned closer. "Please, master. Stand up!"

Pyotr slowly stood up, sheepishly cowering from the cheering audience. Nikolay beckoned him to the stage. Pyotr was much too frightened until Vladimir leaned in and whispered. "Go, master. Take a bow. They love you like I do!"

Finally, Pyotr ambled onto the stage, his clothes rumpled, his face flushed. He was in shock at the outpouring for him and try as he might, managed only a weak, fleeting smile. He bowed, eyes closed, trying to blink away the tears that stung with equal parts joy and disbelief.

SPRING IN MOSCOW SUITED PYOTR JUST FINE. VERY FINE indeed.

The warm evening air of April livened his step as he made his way to the house of his young admirer and gifted pupil, Vladimir Shilovsky. The boy's stepfather was the repertory director of the Moscow's Imperial Theatres and his mother had a passion for the performing arts. The society couple was hosting a party and requested Pyotr join them to help entertain a touring Italian opera company.

While the triumph of his first symphony had quickly faded, and criticism of his work resurged in Petersburg, Pyotr was inspired by everything about Moscow. And, he was determined to prove his doubters wrong. If only he could finish his opera, maybe they would see how they had so harshly misjudged him.

He previewed a section of the first Act at the Bolshoi last month – awkwardly conducting the orchestra himself through the 'Dances of the Chambermaids.' The response was positive, but an opera needed voices. The libretto by his friend Alexander Ostrovsky was inspiring, but at this point only words on paper.

Pyotr knocked on the door of Vladimir's house. There was no response. He knocked again, but when still no one answered he opened it halfway and called out. "Hello?"

Still nothing. "Hello?" he repeated. Then he heard music. A piano... Mozart? 'The Marriage of Figaro'?

And then the purest and most lyrical voice he had ever heard began to sing:

Voi che sapete
che cosa é amor,
Donne, vedete,
s'io l'ho nel cor.

Pyotr let himself in, removed his boots and made his way towards the parlour where a small crowd gathered around a woman wearing a curious head piece of black silk and lace trim. Her small mouth and darting eyes belied the exceptional range of her powerful voice. She stood in front of a gleaming pianoforte.

Her voice cast a spell over Pyotr. Italian opera was dear to him. He even practiced speaking Italian whenever he could and now this intriguing woman, standing just a few feet away, was not only singing in Italian, but singing a Mozart opera.

Sento un affetto,
pien di desir...

'I have a feeling,' he translated silently, 'full of desire.'

Pyotr was frozen, staring at this mesmerizing mezzosoprano who removed her headpiece and began to walk about the room. Her facial expressions conveyed the full range of emotions that hid within Mozart's aria – from raw desire to aching torment.

Ch'ora è diletto,
ch'ora è martir.
Gelo, e poi sento
l'alma avvampar...

Suddenly, her enormous eyes widened even further, her eyebrows raised without missing a beat as she noticed Pyotr. He felt his face warming. She caught his eye as she continued to sing, "I feel my spirit all ablaze!"

He watched her in a trance, and she him, each moving a little closer together as her aria continued. It was as if she were performing only for him.

I flutter and tremble
without knowing why.
I find no peace,
but yet to languish thus
is sheer delight.

She finally turned away, moving gracefully toward the piano to finish the aria. She bowed her head as the small group around her applauded. She raised her doe-like eyes and caught Pyotr staring, slowly clapping his hands in a dream-like stupor.

No woman had bewitched him quite like this before.

"Ladies and gentlemen," a man interrupted the cheering. It was Vladimir Begichev, the stepfather of Pyotr's young admirer, Vladimir. He greeted the woman with a kiss on each cheek. "Our own prima donna soprano, from Belgium, Désirée Artôt."

She took a bow, and someone handed her a flute of champagne. She sipped it, smiling at the outpouring of affection from the room. She whispered something to her host who smiled and waved at Pyotr.

"Mademoiselle Artôt," Begichev announced as Pyotr stepped closer, "may I present Pyotr Ilyich Tchaikovsky, Moscow's best kept musical secret."

Pyotr bowed stiffly. He was not accustomed to the feeling of feminine attraction. His governess Fanny was the only woman, save his mother, who had ever pierced his heart. As a child he dreamed of marrying Fanny, living forever in the warmth of her embrace.

"*Je suis honorée...* Pyotr Ilyich," Désirée purred, "I think perhaps you appreciate *Herr* Mozart as much as I?" Her perfect Russian was sweetened with an alluring French accent, much like Fanny's.

"*Oui, mademoiselle, très certainement,*" he replied, bowing his head. He lifted it slowly, wanting nothing more than to kiss her hand. "Your performance... I have no words that can adequately describe it s... absolute perfection."

She extended her hand, and without thinking, he kneeled and kissed it.

Désirée laughed. "You must come and see my opera, '*Le domino noir.*'"

"I would be more than honoured, what role do you..."

"The soprano, of course!" she interrupted. "I am the lead, Angèle, a novice nun..." she smiled and blinked her eyes somewhat coquettishly, then leaned closer until her lips nearly brushed his. "A nun who has not yet taken her vows."

———

HE KNEW HE WAS A FEW MINUTES EARLY FOR HIS COMPOSITION lesson with young Vladimir, but Pyotr needed a break from the thoughts crashing mercilessly inside his head.

After spending most of July in Paris, he decided it was a city of wonder and delight, but far less suited to a composer than a serene lake in the countryside, a place to deliver his unborn opera, '*The Voyevoda.*' Undoubtedly it would not please his colleagues, that band of Russian composers he called 'The Invincibles,' who preferred originality over beauty. Pyotr argued that Mother Russia would not be served by building a wall around her music.

If only Mademoiselle Désirée Artôt, the hypnotic Belgian mezzo soprano he met in April, would perform his opera. Then, it would soar off the stage. Though he'd left a few short weeks after meeting her for a trip to Berlin and Paris – financed entirely by Vladimir, likely at a cost approaching Pyotr's paltry annual salary – he could not dispatch Désirée from his thoughts.

Her voice was a rich, complex instrument that inspired him to create music equal to its flawless tone.

As he approached the door of Vladimir's suite on the top floor of the hotel, he heard muffled voices and then a loud cry in Russian. "Please, please... don't stop!"

Pyotr froze a few feet from the door. The cry grew into a scream of delicious agony. "Ohhhh... oh, oh... vahhhhhh!"

He approached Vladimir's suite and held his ear to the door. There was only the sound of heavy breathing. Moments later a young man with a smooth but flushed face opened the door. He was no more than twenty. Pyotr stared at the man's surprised expression.

"I was just leaving!" the man said in French. "Aren't you early?"

Pyotr nodded. "Yes, sorry," he mumbled, staring at this elegant creature. Pyotr found himself growing excited, his loins tightening. He cursed his desire to know this man intimately.

"I'm so sorry," Pyotr repeated in a thin voice.

The man touched Pyotr's shoulder. The feeling was electric. Their eyes met briefly and then he walked away, sauntering down the hall like a stallion.

"Come in, master," Vladimir called from inside the room. "I'm ready for my lesson now."

———

IT WAS LATER THAT AFTERNOON BEFORE HE COULD PURGE licentious thoughts of Vladimir's stallion. The screams of pleasure from behind the door kept playing in Pyotr's head. If only he could capture such desire in music – translate Vladimir's noisy ecstasy into the notes and chords of an aria that would rise over an audience, seizing them with its raw passion.

He stood off stage, watching a rehearsal of the Ópera de

Pari's production of Rossini's *Guillaume Tell*. Pyotr was amazed. The costumes, the lighting cues, the simple sets and set changes wondrously transformed the stage with adroit speed and invisible sleight of hand between scenes. No detail, however insignificant, was overlooked. The technical wonders of such staging techniques elevated opera and ballet performances into visual miracles.

As a leading repertory director, his student's father, Vladimir Begichev, was scouting for ideas to bring to Moscow. The younger Vladimir remained in bed at the hotel, apparently too 'tired' to venture out.

"We have no concept of performances such as this," Begichev whispered to Pyotr, as they watched the full dress rehearsal before tonight's premiere. "Imagine our music and their staging, together in Moscow."

"Yes. I've never seen anything quite like it," Pyotr replied. "Look at those costumes, the fine detail, the colours... they seem to glow beneath the limelight. It's truly magical."

Both men watched as the production continued. Even off to the side of the stage, the effect on them was powerful. Afterward, they wandered across the street to a busy café, both lost in their own thoughts.

"How goes your opera?" Begichev finally asked. "Does it sit well with you?"

It was a strange question, Pyotr thought. "Of course not, but I'm feeling inspired of late. Maybe with the right talent..."

"The right soprano?" Begichev offered.

Pyotr nodded.

"You know," Begichev added casually, "she's been asking about you, writing to me, hoping to see you again."

"Who?" Pyotr touched his beard. "Désirée?"

"Of course!" Begichev replied. "She's coming to Moscow in the autumn for another tour." He reached for his cup. "This might be an opportunity for you to..." he hesitated. He finished his coffee and set the cup down slowly.

"To what?" Pyotr implored.

"To prove yourself."

Pyotr stiffened. "As a composer, you mean?"

Begichev sat up in his chair. "Yes, but also... as a man."

BACK HOME AFTER A SHORT VISIT WITH HIS BROTHERS MODEST and Anatoly in Estonia, late autumn was not quite done with Moscow.

Nor was Moscow done with Pyotr.

"This is your commission?" Nikolay asked as he leafed through the papers on top of Pyotr's bureau. Both men were dressed elegantly for tonight's gala performance of 'Le domino noir,' at the Bolshoi in honour of Désirée Artôt.

"It is, indeed," Pyotr responded, searching for his top hat. "Just some additional choruses and recitatives for pianoforte."

"Mademoiselle will be pleased," Nikolay smiled. "And I believe you will be too. I was asked by the company's impresario, Signore Merelli, to find a suitable pianist for your work."

Pyotr eyed his friend, his landlord and if truth be told, his protector, with a wary eye. Nikolay Rubinstein had given him a job teaching at the conservatory, provided free room and board and acted much like an older brother. And could be just as annoying.

Even if Nikolay's guidance was sound, Pyotr preferred to find his own road.

"Really? I was not aware of that," Pyotr finally responded. Merelli had paid fifty rubles for the commission – fifty precious rubles which Pyotr should have used to pay off one of his many debts coming due this month if he was not so foolish with his money.

"Are you not curious who I found to play your music?" Nikolay prodded as they donned their coats and footwear for the short walk to the theatre.

"Provided they are proficient and disciplined in their technique, I will be more than satisfied," Pyotr responded as they left the house.

"I believe you shall be..." Nikolay whispered with a smile.

At the theatre, a flush rose to Pyotr's cheeks when he spotted Désirée.

They had become good friends since her return to Moscow last month. Though she was not a striking beauty, her voice – both its dramatic quality and exceptional range – cast a glow around her, made even brighter by her unwavering artistic dedication. He knew how hard she strove to perfect the poetry of her vocal interpretations.

"Is it true what Signore Merelli told me this morning?" she asked as they stood at the foot of the stage near the edge of the orchestra pit. "You've written new works for the opera?"

"I have, Mademoiselle." He hesitated. "I do hope it pleases," he moved a little closer, "everyone."

Désirée touched his arm. "I know it will." She let her hand linger a moment. He longed to be one with her, two artists joined in musical union. This might be the purest form of love he could ever hope to find in a woman.

"Pyotr Ilyich!" a booming voice interrupted.

He turned, startled to see the face of his old professor from the Saint Petersburg conservatory, Anton Rubinstein, Nikolay's older brother.

"Anton?" Pyotr fumbled, "What? Why are you..."

"I invited him," Nikolay cut in, striding over from the orchestra pit. "I was told to find a 'competent' pianist, and, this is the best I could find!"

"I am deeply honoured," Pyotr finally managed to blurt out. "Are you playing..."

"Your music?" Anton laughed. He pulled a sheet of music from his jacket. "I am. It's brilliant. I will try to be true to its exceptionality."

Anton was better than his word. His playing was divine,

creating musical emotions that Pyotr could hardly believe had sprung from his own pen. And Désirée was inspired too, performing her part as Angèle as if delivering the final act of her career.

From her entrance to her final scene, it was obvious she was born for the stage. Her natural talent as an actress was obvious – as was her extraordinary vocal range and ability to play both tragic and comedic parts. The rich timbre of her voice, more oboe than flute, was filled with warmth and passion.

Pyotr melted into his seat watching her. He was falling in love with her as a performer and perhaps, even as a woman.

It mattered not which one was true.

HIS FATHER WAS BESIDE HIMSELF WITH NEWS THAT PYOTR WAS enraptured by a woman whom his son described as possessing exquisite grace of movement and artistic poise. Never was there a kinder or cleverer woman, he wrote to Papa.

"If you are serious, there is only one question I would ask you. Do you love each other truly, and for all time?" his father replied. "If the answer be yes, turn your affair into an offer of marriage. Make capital of both your talents! Two musical artists could give birth to a family of gifted grandchildren."

He read the letter from dear sweet *Papochka* again. "A family of gifted children."

Pyotr smiled. Marriage and a family would serve him well, make Papa proud, and quell any rumours of Pyotr's unorthodox urges. Maybe he could find fulfillment in the arms of a woman whose artistry defined her. He told his brothers he had never experienced such powerful artistic passion as he did when he was in the company of Désirée.

Closing his eyes at night he saw her on stage, the aura of her perfection floating into his dreams.

But he was wide awake at the moment. He was preparing for

his daily visit to Désirée's house, where hopefully her mother, who continually chaperoned her daughter's every move, might be persuaded to attend to her own business for an hour or two.

He wanted to be alone when he proposed marriage and made their betrothal official.

Pyotr looked over the papers on his bureau. He shivered with the apprehension of so much hurry-scurry work to complete. He needed to finish the last of more than two dozen Russian folk songs for four hands that he had been obsessing over for weeks. He also wanted to revise sections of his new work, '*Fatum*' a symphonic fantasia in C minor. And his opera, '*The Voyevoda*,' required urgent attention.

At a choral rehearsal of it last month, he had undertaken the pianoforte accompaniment himself. The singers were pleased, but he was not yet happy with the opera. Perhaps when he returned tonight, a betrothed man no less, he would revise the remaining sections that still weren't right.

As he was about to leave, there was a knock on the front door. He opened it, and a striking young man stood tall in the doorway.

"Pyotr Ilyich?" the man asked in a reverent tone. He held a violin case. His face seemed familiar.

"Yes. May I help you?"

"Have you but a few moments, maestro? I have a patron who thinks we might work together on a commission."

Pyotr studied the man. His neatly trimmed moustache, his impeccable grooming, fine attire, and just the faintest hint of an aromatic cologne combined into a most appealing package.

A light mist was beginning to fall through the chill of a December evening. "Would you like to step inside?" Pyotr offered. "But first tell me, why do you seem so familiar?"

"I am second violin, under Nikolay's baton most evenings," the man replied and bowed his head slightly. "I am Iosif. I joined your composition class last week at the conservatory." He lowered his eyes to the ground. "I have taken to playing the *scherzo* from your 'Daydreams of a Winter Journey' almost every evening, if I may be so bold as to reveal to you."

Pyotr touched his mouth, unsure how to respond to such a statement. "Thank you," he said weakly. "Come in, Iosif."

With Nikolay gone to visit friends for the weekend, Pyotr felt free to invite Iosif to make himself comfortable. Besides his violin, Iosif carried a bottle of red wine which he offered as a gift. It was not long before they opened it, and Pyotr savoured the rich, black cherry notes of the wine, followed by the even sweeter ones of Iosif's violin.

The man seemed to know every piece of music Pyotr had ever composed.

"Your style is both original and traditional," Iosif mused after he laid down his bow and sipped his wine. "You neither bow to German masters nor snub Russian innovators. You have found a way to pay homage to both, while creating something entirely your own."

His words were like a soothing balm. "Not many share your view, but thank you." Pyotr removed his jacket and finished his wine. "Tell me about this patron who wants us to work together."

Iosif smiled. "Actually, our patron wishes to remain anonymous, but offers one hundred rubles to each of us. We can choose the form." He bent over and picked up a sheet of paper from inside his violin case. "I thought perhaps... a violin concerto?"

He handed Pyotr the paper. It was sheet music with a simple structure. "It's not much, but this came to me one night after... well, after I dreamed of a dance set to your music."

"A dance?" Pyotr laughed. He studied the music and the notes beside the first bar. "Pizzicato?"

"I pinch the strings... it creates a kind of dreamy quality, a child-like innocence." Iosif plucked the strings of his violin and indeed the sound was like that of a fairy creature not quite of this world, tender and sweet with promise.

"I like it, Iosif," Pyotr said softly. He was finding it hard to remain in his seat much longer. He wanted to get to know this man, completely. "And I ... I..." he couldn't be sure, but there seemed to be a mutual interest.

Iosif put down his violin and stood before Pyotr. "It's not only music that draws me to you."

PYOTR SAT STIFFLY ACROSS FROM DÉSIRÉE ARTÔT AS SHE prepared tea and arranged pastries on a platter.

Last evening had been a wondrous mixture of musical discovery with Iosif.

Though they had openly shared their desire for each other, Pyotr had fought to keep the evening platonic, and mostly managed to abide by that limitation. After they had completed nearly fifty bars of a concerto for piano and violin, they were exhausted. Iosif left as dawn was breaking, leaving Pyotr with a tender kiss and a promise he would wait for a chance to be with him, no matter how long it took.

"What happened to you last night, my darling?" Désirée asked as she sat down beside him. "I was expecting you, and Mama was out too!" she winked.

"I'm sorry, my dear." He chose his words carefully. "I was working... working on a new commission. It could form the basis of an aria for you."

She touched his hand and kissed his cheek. "You are so thoughtful. Perhaps you could come to Warsaw with us and I could audition it for the Poles."

He flinched. All his friends, particularly Nikolay Rubinstein, warned him that he would be the feeblest of husbands if he married Désirée. He would be required to follow her to all the corners of Europe like a pet on a leash, living off the scraps of the income she threw him, with little opportunity to compose.

"My dear, you know I love your heart and soul and feel I

cannot live without you but," Pyotr hesitated. "If we marry, I would plead with you to come and live here in Moscow with me. My career is just starting and..."

"Mine already brings fame and fortune!" she interrupted. "I do love you so, Pyotr. But I could never give up the stages of Paris, London, Berlin and..." Désirée stopped. "Wait, are you proposing to me, my darling?" She took his hand. "I accept!"

Before he could say anything more, Désirée's mother marched into the room holding something in her hand. She towed a man behind her and Pyotr was shocked to see it was his companion from last night, Iosif.

"Leave us," she said firmly to her daughter. "Please check on preparations for tonight's banquet. I have business to discuss with these gentlemen."

"But, Mama..." Désirée started to protest.

"Leave us."

Désirée rose without another word and strode out of the room like a wounded peacock. Her mother closed the door behind her and plunked herself down in the armchair across from Pyotr. Iosif stood uneasily beside her.

"Sit!" she ordered him.

He took a seat beside Pyotr, avoiding his eyes.

Désirée's mother was a refined woman of advancing years. Her hair was impossibly black despite her age, her makeup heavy and pale in contrast.

"I know about you two," she said coldly. "What you are, and what perversions you try to hide."

Neither man spoke, but Pyotr thought he could hear Iosif's heart pounding.

She threw down a copy of the concerto Pyotr and Iosif had worked on last night. "This is the work of the devil. I know from my spy that you spent last night together. My scheme worked as I feared it might. But at least now I know the truth."

There was a moment of silence, like that between sections of a tragic opera.

"I will not bring scandal upon my daughter," she said. Her eyes scanned both men, their heads bowed. "Pyotr Ilyich, before I break her heart, tell me that what I believe about you is not true. Tell me that I am wrong... about you."

Pyotr looked over at Iosif. Tears loomed in his eyes and Iosif looked for all the world like a man broken into pieces that might never be put back together again.

"No madam," Pyotr finally responded. "You are not wrong about me."

CHAPTER 6

To call the process of composing his first symphony an ordeal for Pyotr Ilyich Tchaikovsky would be an understatement.

'Winter Daydreams,' as the work was subtitled, gave the composer a severe nervous breakdown. He spent days and nights working on it, suffered from insomnia and a lack of creative energies due to this. This exhaustion, combined with the harsh criticism from his former teachers, and the struggle of writing within the formal structures of the symphony-form, must have made the compositional process an excruciating one at best. Nevertheless, it remained one of his personal favourite works, perhaps in part due to the long arduous road he travelled for it.

A symphony, in today's meaning, is a large, complex musical work, generally written for the orchestra. In its most common form, it consists of four movements (though three movement symphonies were customary well into the 18th century).

The first movement is often found to be in sonata form, a structure that contains an exposition, development and then recapitulation. Thematic material is introduced in the exposition, elaborated upon in the development, then brought back and resolved in the recapitulation. It often follows an overall 'plan', following a structure of modulation from tonic key to dominant, statement of musical ideas and their reaffirmation.

Repeating structures are often employed (such as a coda) to strengthen a sense of resolution in the piece. In Tchaikovsky's 'Winter Daydreams', this first movement is in G minor, with 'allegro tranquillo' as the chosen tempo (fast and calm).

The second movement tends to be a slower one; in the case of 'Winter Daydreams', a movement labelled *adagio cantabile, ma non tanto*(slowly and songlike, but not so much), contrasting against the often faster first movement.

The third movement of the symphony tends to be a faster dance form, most commonly the minuet and trio, though many composers such as Beethoven employed a somewhat livelier form called 'scherzo'. In Winter Daydreams, the third movement is a scherzo.

The fourth and final movement of the symphony often welcomes back an allegro or sonata form, though the rondo form (a form where thematic material is restated, interjected with contrasting material) is not uncommon. In the case of Tchaikovsky's first symphony, this last section develops from *andante* (moderately slow) to a majestic *allegro* (fast), ending the symphony in G major (a common choice in works starting in a minor key).

All of these forms come with their own characteristics, some of them quite detailed. For example, the recapitulation in the sonata form is often in the tonic key of the piece, and thematic material that has not been previously stated in the tonic key now does so, allowing them to resolve. In the exposition, the second section is often found to be in the dominant key (if the first section was in a major key), or the relative major if the first section was in a minor key.

To give a full analysis of the symphony form would be well beyond the scope of this book, and many excellent works exist on the subject where interested readers can find further details.

Suffice to say that composing a symphony is not only a challenge of scale (a duration of 45 or more minutes is quite common), but also of structure and cohesion, and most certainly of creativity. Writing such an enormous piece for a full orchestra requires mastery of musical theory and practice in order to succeed.

WORKING AROUND THE RULES

It is not hard to see why this work would have been such a challenge to Tchaikovsky (or indeed any composer). Tchaikovsky also found himself struggling somewhat with the form and 'rules' of the sonata form, feeling that they were more of a hindrance in the creative process than an aid.

The manner of exposition, development and treatment of thematic material in a way that could have been heard from Haydn or Mozart, did not suit him or his particular talent as a composer, and he was forced to find a way to work around these rules in a manner that was suitable to his particular musical genius. However, other factors were in play that complicated his work even further.

Even though the symphony had not yet been finished, Tchaikovsky decided to show it to his former teachers Rubinstein and Zaremba. His hope was that they would consider the work suitable for performance in one of the Russian Musical Society concerts in Saint Petersburg. This hope was quickly dashed when both Rubinstein and Zaremba spoke critically and harshly of the work, and the work was most definitely not approved for performance.

Both Rubinstein and Zaremba were conservative in their personal tastes, and both strived to preserve what they considered to be the best in Western tradition. Both looked very fondly upon the musical styles from German masters such as Bach, Haydn and Mendelssohn. In this style, a certain strictness to the governing rules of counterpoint and harmony can be found, and they considered this to be the legacy of Western musical tradition that they wished to uphold. With this in mind, Zaremba's judgement of Tchaikovsky work as 'not being German or Russian, and not pleasing to either', takes more solid form.

They were not impressed or amused by the creative liberties that Tchaikovsky had taken in the draft of his symphony where these clashed with the more traditional ideas of harmony and counterpoint at the time and judged the work to be inappropriate for performance. Zaremba even went so far as insisting Tchaikovsky compose a new second subject in the first movement. With Tchaikovsky's style leaning much stronger towards romanticism and a looser application of the rules of strict counterpoint and harmony, the symphony represented a change in musical trend that both Zaremba and Rubinstein were quite hostile against.

For Tchaikovsky, who had throughout his life heard such judgement before and no doubt had it lingering in the back of his mind while working on 'Winter Daydreams', receiving such harsh criticism only reinforced his fears of failing at the composition of a symphony. After all the hard work he had put in, and the emotional and physical toll the work had taken on him, being rejected so cruelly by his former teachers was more than a bit disheartening. Their influence on the possibility of having the work performed forced him to revise the work. Unfortunately, even with extensive revisions to meet the conditions of reconsidering the work for performance, both did not approve of the work as a whole, instead approving only the second and third movement.

Both movements were finally performed in 1867 at one of the Russian Musical Society concerts, but were not given a warm reception by their audience. The whole symphony would not be performed until 1868. Between the performances of the two movements in 1867 and the full symphony in 1868, Tchaikovsky discarded much of the revisions he had been forced to make by

Zaremba and Rubinstein, frustrated by their criticism and the less than warm welcome the first two movements had received in 1867. In hindsight, this decision to follow his own creativity and style was exactly the right thing to do; the performance of the full symphony in 1868 was met with great success.

CHAPTER 7

MOSCOW, FEBRUARY, 1869 (AGE 29)

The stage of the Bolshoi theatre was hardly large enough to hold the egos of all the operatic performers rehearsing upon it. And even with its deep orchestra pit, it was certainly no match when the composer, choreographer and the wardrobe director were added.

All were in a heightened state of agitation with less than forty-eight hours before the curtain rose on the premiere of Pyotr's first opera, *The Voyevoda*.

He massaged his tired eyes as the baritone and tenor argued with the conductor about the last scene of Act Two. Their fight had lost meaning to him – a cacophony of noise without form or tempo. They had begun their dress rehearsal late this afternoon and it had now dragged on for more than nine hours. Though mentally drained, Pyotr had to find a way to complete the rehearsal.

"Quiet!" he finally screeched. "Enough!"

All eyes turned to him in the wings where he stood seething. He scanned the stage, searching the faces of the performers until he landed on Aleksandra Menshikova. She bowed her head reverently, long wispy bangs of her dark hair falling low over her face.

"Everyone, off the stage, now!" he barked. "Everyone except... Aleksandra"

The soprano glanced up smiling. She locked her hands together as the other performers and crew shuffled off the stage muttering to themselves as the forlorn eyes of the orchestra followed their departure.

"Now, let's hear 'The Nightingale' song, one more time before we move on to Act Three," Pyotr requested, pointing to the conductor who released a long sigh before directing his baton to the clarinet section and raising his hand toward the strings.

Bright notes from the clarinets rose innocently, with the support of lush violins and violas. On stage, Aleksandra swept back her hair, took two steps forward and began to fill the Bolshoi with a sound that made Pyotr tremble. She was *his* voice, almost as perfect as his dear Désirée. He closed his eyes a moment and for a split second, the woman who had cast such a spell over him was back on stage, serenading Pyotr like a betrothed songbird about to take flight.

He opened his eyes returning to the Bolshoi, watching and listening as Aleksandra found the shape of each note and phrase, transforming Pyotr's score into a work of musical sublimity.

Someone came up behind Pyotr and laid a hand on his shoulder. He glanced back to see Nikolay Rubenstein, carrying a heavy face.

Aleksandra finished with an exalted note that she held until it transcended above everyone in the Bolshoi and then delicately evaporated. A spontaneous round of applause and cheering followed.

"Thank you, Aleksandra," Pyotr called out. "I am forever in your debt."

She bowed her head, turned and headed off stage.

"I have news from Warsaw," Nikolay whispered, holding a piece of paper in his hand. "A telegram, from Désirée Artôt."

Pyotr blinked. Her separation had been sudden, less than six weeks ago. Despite their issues, her absence had left something of a hole inside him. No other woman had touched his heart like her, and his dream of a union with such a perfect artist was something he refused to concede.

"I'm tired, Nikolay. Please, can you read it to me?" Pyotr sighed. "Is it good n..."

"She was married last night," Nikolay interrupted, "to a Spaniard... in her opera company."

"What?" Pyotr cried, grabbing the telegram. He scanned it quickly:

Pyotr Ilyich, my dearest. I was married last night to Mariano Padilla y Ramos.
You are released from our arrangement.

"No! No!" he gasped. "This must be a trick, a scheme... by her mother!"

Nikolay shook his head. "Ramos is a baritone in their company. They've sung together for years." He paused a moment, nodding his head. "I noticed how she seemed to favour him when they performed here last month."

"Really?" Pyotr snapped. "She told me he was a boy with a lisp, not even a man."

There was no response from Nikolay who simply shrugged.

Pyotr could not find words for his rage. He held his breath, his face warming.

"Ready to begin Act Three?" the conductor called out from the orchestra pit. The performers had gathered on stage and were taking up their positions.

Pyotr crushed the telegram in his fist, turned on his heel and strode from the theatre without another word.

THE HAZY AIR IN THE PRIVATE CLUB CLOAKED THE GROUP OF men hidden together behind faceless iron doors.

They sat in small groups, drinking and smoking. Muffled laughter and a sense of intimate gaiety permeated the atmosphere, cloaked from the prying eyes of respectable Moscow.

Pyotr stormed into the club chased by a dark cloud of despair. He didn't want to think – only to feel.

A voice called out to him. "Master!"

Vladimir Shilovsky stood up from a table and waved. "The rehearsal's over?"

Pyotr nodded. He was nearly frozen from the frigid February night air. He brushed snow from his shoulder and covered his eyes with his hands, warming the tiny icicles that had formed on his eyelashes.

"Something wrong?" Vladimir asked quietly as he approached.

Pyotr groaned. Behind him, someone helped take off his overcoat and top hat. He turned to take in a familiar face, Eduard Sack, a tall student from his composition class at the Moscow Conservatory.

"Thank you," Pyotr whispered, studying the boy's smooth face.

"Join us, master," Vladimir said. "Come, sit... we just ordered a bottle." He pointed to a small table and motioned for Pyotr to take a seat.

Vladimir poured drinks as they each lit cigarettes. In the corner, a piano played a languid, wandering tune, offering a sultry theme as smoky as the room itself. The vodka burned Pyotr's throat as the notes of the music drifted around him onto a treble clef in his mind.

"Are you as excited as I am for Saturday?" Vladimir asked, refilling their glasses. "Your first opera, and at the Bolshoi, too!" He picked up his glass and Eduard raised his as well. "A toast, to our gifted professor – our inspiration!"

Pyotr drank down his vodka and stared blankly at his two admirers, but could not force a smile to take possession of his face.

Vladimir reached across the table. "Do you not wish to celebrate... with us?"

Pyotr reached into the pocket of his jacket and grabbed the crumpled telegraph. "It's not you," he replied, scanning the short note again. "It's her, the one I lost."

"Lost?" Vladimir asked. "Who?"

Looking away, Pyotr handed him the telegram. Vladimir read it, then handed it to Eduard who stared at it a moment before speaking.

"I heard you were to be married," he said quietly. "Was she in your heart, truly?"

"I thought she was... yes," Pyotr replied. This boy, Eduard, had such compassion written across his face. It was so plain, especially in his eyes. Pyotr felt like he needed to explain more. "Her voice... it was as if God had found a vessel for me to worship, a way to share myself with the world through her."

He sighed and added quietly. "I was quite prepared to enter hymen's bonds."

Eduard reached down under the table, pulled a weathered volume from his satchel, and laid it on the table. "True love and tragedy," he whispered, as if revealing a dark secret, "they are always eternal companions."

He pushed the volume toward Pyotr who scanned the title: *Romeo and Juliet* by William Shakespeare.'

At this Pyotr finally smiled. "Thank you, Eduard." He studied the cover of the book, set in a font and style reminiscent of a bygone age.

"Pain is the greatest gift an artist can receive," Eduard added, laying a hand on Pyotr. "Don't waste it."

FIVE YEARS LATER...
Moscow, December 1874 (Age 34)

THE IRON GRATE ON PYOTR'S BRICK STOVE REMAINED OPEN, even after he finished stoking it with three scoops of coal from the scuttle. For good measure, he threw in a birch log to incite more flames.

The brightness and warmth from the stove provided only fleeting comfort against his dark cold thoughts.

He glanced over at the clock; nearly nine o'clock in the evening. The two Nikolay's – Rubenstein and Hubert – would soon be here to hear him perform his first piano concerto. Since he had begun writing it just eight weeks ago it had taken on a life of its own making. Had he finally found his wings?

This piece flowed from his pen as quickly as he could transcribe it onto paper. Would it please the two professionals he most admired – two men who could also reduce him to jelly with their sharp tongues?

No matter what they said, he was determined he would not change a single note this time.

The flames from the stove jumped higher, and for a moment he considered putting the grate back in place.

Nyet, he warned himself sternly.

On his desk he had organized all the music he had ever composed into two piles; all original, signed copies. On top of the first lay the cover page of *Fatum,* the tone poem Mily Balakirev had conducted five years ago. And afterward, savaged with criticism so fierce, Pyotr had almost been inclined to give up on composition and focus his musical ambitions on reviewing the work of others and tutoring students.

The top sheet of the other pile was the cover to his *Romeo and Juliet* overture. He picked up the sheet of music, his eyes growing moist. He couldn't forget the expression on the face of Eduard Sack when he heard Pyotr play this piece on the piano.

It was summer, one year ago – the last time Pyotr saw him. Three months later, Eduard put a pistol in his mouth and blew his brains out.

IT WAS LATE JULY. PYOTR THOUGHT BACK TO THAT DAY WHEN Eduard revealed himself and finally laid bare his feelings...

Eduard and Pyotr sat near the front of the theatre with a small group of drama students. The young actors on stage held them entranced as they channelled the power of Shakespeare's words.

Romeo knows not that the sleeping draught Juliet had taken only makes her *seem* dead. Grief-stricken; he reaches for his own poison so he can join her. The actor playing Romeo turned to Eduard and Pyotr sitting near the front of the theatre.

"Death, that hath sucked the honey of thy breath,
Hath had no power yet upon thy beauty.
Thou art not conquered. Beauty's ensign yet
Is crimson in thy lips and in thy cheeks,
O true apothecary,
Thy drugs are quick. Thus with a kiss I die."

Romeo kissed the young woman playing Juliet and then with an exaggerated flourish, drank the coloured liquid from the small vial he held, gasped and fell beside Juliet. Moments later she awoke to find her true love dead.

There was a long silence when the production was over, followed by hearty applause. Afterward, Pyotr and Eduard walked together saying little to each other. Eduard had unexpectedly showed up in Moscow a few days ago, and Pyotr had helped arrange for him to attend the student production of *Romeo and Juliet.*

"Thank you," Eduard finally spoke as the two men wandered towards the park near the river Moskva, "I understand now that I am not alone."

Without understanding completely, Pyotr felt a kinship with the words. "Let's sit a while," he replied. "Enjoy the summer air."

They found a bench with a view of the river, beneath a towering ash tree. Although daylight was fading, the soft glow of moonlight would not be long in taking its place. Pyotr turned to Eduard. "Help me understand, Eduard."

"You can call me Edya," he replied. "And know that I am yours, completely."

Despite the feelings that Pyotr had been fighting, the words flowed straight to his heart. He knew though, that going any further with a boy of nineteen, a student almost half his age, would bring even more scandal. Rubinstein and others whom he respected, warned that his relationships with young men would ruin his career. The disconcerting talk and gossip was becoming louder each day.

"You know..." Pyotr replied slowly, "Edya, I do very much want to be with you, but we can never be."

"Yes, I understand. It's why I know I am not long for this world." Eduard touched Pyotr's hand and let it rest there. The warmth of Eduard's touch was overwhelming. "I will come to violence, but...." he hesitated. "But..."

Pyotr put his other hand over Eduard's. He leaned closer. The pain from this young man was excruciating. "But what?"

"I want to know you first," he pleaded. He looked toward the river and added quietly. "I love you."

Now real pain shot through Pyotr. How could this be? And could he deny that he did not feel the same?

"No, Edya, no please, do not say that." Pyotr turned away, trying not to break down into tears. "I can't... cannot be with you."

The boy nodded. His eyes glistened. "I understand, but could I ask you, please... Just one kiss? And then I will be forever gone."

AS HE FINISHED THE RECITAL OF HIS FIRST PIANO CONCERTO, Pyotr closed his eyes and Eduard's beautifully haunting face stared at him warmly.

Edya is pleased.

Pyotr reached the end of the last bar of his new composition and let his hands remain on the keys of the piano. He lowered his head, then slowly turned toward the two Nikolay's. Their expressions were blank.

The room was deadly silent.

"Well?" Pyotr asked, slowly rising from the piano.

"I'm sorry to say, but that was no good," Nikolay Rubinstein finally spoke, his dry pursed lips parting at last. "It's almost impossible to play well, so many awkward passages so..."

The other Nikolay said nothing. But in his silence there was even greater disdain.

"Poorly composed," Rubinstein added. "It would be almost impossible to correct it all." His face made a sour expression. "I found it vulgar." He shook his head in a kind of pitiful rebuke. "Your First Piano Concerto? I expected more from you."

"Did you steal bits from here, there and everywhere?" Rubinstein continued, his scorn rising into a fever pitch, almost like Jove the Thunderer. "Such a trivial, common work... broken, disconnected. Unplayable!"

Pyotr rose from his chair and left the room, leaving his critics to stew in their contempt. He stood outside the door gathering himself. He thought this would be easier by now. He was wrong.

Never lay your soul bare unless you're prepared to absorb the thorns of rejection.

He breathed deeply, furious at the two men on the other side of the door, but even more angry with himself. He took another laboured breath, opened the door and walked back inside.

Without a word, Pyotr reached for the first stack of music and grabbed a few sheets from the top of the pile. He moved toward the flames of the open stove and threw the pages inside.

"Burn in hell, *Fatum*," he cried.

"Pyotr!" Rubinstein cried. "What are you doing?"

"Ridding the world of my 'appalling cacophony' of a 'form that does not work,' a thing 'completely uncoordinated'." Pyotr snapped. "To quote your most high holiness of music!"

"But, that," he stammered, "was before you changed..."

"You were right the first time. It does not deserve to live." Pyotr took the remainder of the score that his 'friends' so soundly rejected and threw it into the stove. The flames roared higher with the added fuel – the only copies of the original scores, his musical sins he needed to erase from posterity by sending them to hell.

Nikolay stood up from his chair. "Pyotr Ilyich, you're being stupid. We recognize your talent. We're only here to help!"

Pyotr snorted. He reached for the title page to his opera, *The Voyevoda*. He held it up for Nikolay.

"Were you trying to help when you pulled my opera after only five performances?" He threw the page into the fire. "Your *help* is no longer needed."

With that he gathered together the remaining sheet music for the opera, cast them into the stove and watched as the flames erased his musical imperfections from the world forever.

CHAPTER 8

T chaikovsky did play his first piano concerto to Nikolay Rubinstein (younger brother to Anton Rubinstein) and pianist Nikolay Hubert. As Tchaikovsky himself was not a pianist, he considered the input of the two piano virtuosos vital to understand which parts of his work would require attention for playability and technicality. Though it's likely that he expected a fair bit of criticism, not just on the technical piano performance parts, Rubinstein's outburst was more severe than anticipated.

There are a few possible explanations for Rubinstein's reaction. As was often the case with his works, Tchaikovsky made certain choices regarding harmony and structure that deviated from the established Western (German) tradition. Instead of repeating the grandiose first theme throughout the piece, as audiences had come to expect, he introduced new themes. The thunderous and dramatic first movement had little counterbalance in the rest of the piece, especially the last movement, which was much lighter than the first.

Also, ears accustomed to obvious interconnectedness between the piano parts during movements may find this composition somewhat loose and disjointed upon hearing the piece for the first time. Whether any or all of these issues were the reason for Rubinstein's outburst is hard to say. One cannot help but wonder what revisions would have come from his feedback had Rubinstein delivered it in a more friendly and supportive manner. However, his tantrum had the opposite effect, causing Tchaikovsky to swear adamantly not to change a single note (though he would make revisions to the piece later in his life).

The criticism we saw in earlier chapters that Tchaikovsky's work sounded 'neither German, nor Russian' was drawn from several occasions in his life. Anton Rubinstein in particular had expressed his displeasure at this ambiguity, favouring the more traditional German practices himself. Within Russia, reforms had been underway for a long time to "modernise" the country, which in practice involved the import of many aspects of Western culture into the Russian one, music included.

A conflict arose between those who disagreed on the direction Russian classical music should take. Composers like Rubinstein drew heavily on Western practices and traditions, while composers such as Mily Balakirev strove for musical nationalism, attempting to create a distinct Russian style of classical music, drawing on elements of daily Russian life.

Balakirev was an incredibly talented musician and pianist. His work 'Islamey' remains famous amongst pianists and audiences alike, a virtuosic and fiendishly difficult piano work. Around 1856-1862, a group of composers gathered around Balakirev with the intention of developing a Russian style of music that would be authentic to the country and its heritage, and in doing so stop the Western influences that were infiltrating the Russian culture.

An important role model for them was Mikhail Glinka, who drew heavily on folk songs and experiences from his youth, such as peasant choirs. Glinka had travelled through Europe extensively before deciding on his return to Russia to champion the Russian musical style. His works and the techniques he used served as inspiration to this group of composers in further development in the Russian style. The group (sometimes referred to as 'The Five' or 'The Mighty Handful') included César Cui, Nikolai Rimsky-Korsakov, Alexander Borodino, Modest Mussorgsky and, of course, Mily Balakirev, who was considered the driving force of the group, and its founder.

RUSSIA VERSUS THE WEST

The Russian style developed and championed by Balakirev and his compatriots employed several techniques that set it apart from the Western style, drawing from Russian folk songs, church music and folk dances.

One example of such distinctive techniques was the shifting nature of tonality compared to the more 'stable' Western style. Tonality refers to the way a piece is structured around a central note or key, and the harmonic relations to that note.

In the Western style, the tonic is the starting note of a scale; so a C major scale has C as its tonic. The chords created on the individual notes of this scale have a clear relation to the tonic. An important relationship is "the dominant" note, which is five steps above the start of the scale. For example, in a C major scale, the note G is the dominant, and chords that start with G are considered dominant chords. When hearing a triad (a chord made of three notes, each two notes apart) that starts with G while listening to a piece in the key of C major, those accustomed to the Western style will come to expect a return to C, the tonic. So strong is this convention of the dominant function in our ears, we have a sense that all is "right"when we progress from the dominant G chord to the tonic C.

For every note in the scale there is a corresponding function and relationship to the tonic C. Because of this, even if we are unaware of the underlying theory, we are guided as listeners through the piece and come to expect certain moments of resolve and repose. Skillful composers can take advantage of such expectations by postponing resolution to the tonal centre (the tonic C in the above example) to keep us in suspense.

In the Russian style promoted by Balakirev and fellows, this tonal centre was much more shifting and elusive. Because of this, harmonic progressions and functions seem to lack a sense of auditory logic to many Western ears, as our expectations aren't met, and we are seemingly denied a stable frame of tonal reference. Even when skilfully executed by composers such as Balakirev, these seemingly unstable and unpredictable twists and turns in a piece will at first be confusing to the Western ear.

Another sharp contrast in the Russian style is the use of parallel fourths and fifths, that is, sounding two simultaneous notes four or five steps apart and then moving them up or down the scale. . These progressions have a very distinct character and can sound somewhat unpleasant to Western ears. In earlier forms of Western counterpoint, such progressions were even forbidden. This isn't to say that Western composers didn't occasionally employ them on purpose to create a jarring effect, but still such use was fairly limited compared to its Russian counterpart. Even in modern Western music theory, students are warned against using parallel fifths and encouraged to find a less obtrusive resolution in their harmony.

These and other techniques were derived from Russian folk songs, dances, and church music, as stated earlier. But Balakirev's group also added various harmonic techniques to their Russian style that had no basis in these forms of traditional Russian music at all. They did so consciously to create a Russian classical style to counteract the Western influences that had been creeping up on their cultural heritage. Such added techniques included the usage of the whole tone scale, as opposed to the major and minor scale more commonly found in Western classical music. Glinka had already used this scale to good effect in his works, and it was used by many Russian composers (including Tchaikovsky) for its distinct sound. In later years, Claude

Debussy would also employ the whole tone scale abundantly in his works, which lent them their dreamlike nature. Modern audiences will have heard eerie sounding film scores based on the whole tone scale.

The pentatonic scale also became part of the Russian classical style as developed by The Five. Whereas the major and minor scale employ seven notes in one octave, the pentatonic scale uses only five. Its sound suggests an Eastern element, and this was a strong characteristic of The Five's style. Balakirev in particular encouraged using Eastern elements and harmony to further distinguish the Russian classical style from its Western counterpart.

Tchaikovsky's choice of a Ukranian folk song as melody in his piano concerto must have put a smile on Balakirev's face. But despite numerous attempts by Balakirev and others to get him to join their movement, Tchaikovsky would drift in between the two 'camps' for the rest of his life. It is, perhaps, one of the characteristics of his style that served to broaden its appeal to future audiences.

CHAPTER 9

MOSCOW, MAY 1875 (AGE 35)

The young boy sat in silence at the dining room table, his mouth pursed in a flat line that was neither frown nor smile. A spark of curiosity in his wide eyes countered his aloof demeanour, as his gaze shifted back and forth between Pyotr sitting across him from and Modest sitting beside him.

"Modi," Pyotr asked, using the endearment he preferred for his young brother, "please, tell me how to communicate with him if he cannot hear or speak. And, remind me, what is his name?"

"Nikolay Konradi, but I call him 'Kolya'," Modest replied. "His parents have given up hope for his future, and even they don't know how to communicate with him. He was born deaf and mute, but now that he is seven, I think maybe I can..."

Pyotr waited for his brother to finish. Modest and Kolya had arrived early this morning by train. After a hearty breakfast of kasha porridge, boiled eggs and toast with fresh cheese, they now sat together finishing tea drawn from the polished copper samovar at the end of the dining room table.

"You think what?" Pyotr asked. "That there might yet be some promise for little Kolya?"

"I do. I think that's why his parents hired me as his tutor," Modest replied. "I see a glimmer in his eyes. Watch."

Modest placed his hand on the boy's head and began to chant like a monk, droning over and over.

The boy's face brightened; his brown eyes widened. Pushing his lips together, Kolya made a low sound. "Hummm. Baaaa. Ohhhhhhh-kkk."

Pyotr gasped. "Is he trying to... to talk?"

"Yes! He can make many different sounds," Modest beamed. "He is so smart! And I'm teaching him to read and write too."

Modest handed Kolya a pen and a scrap of paper. The boy began to write. When he finished, he held it up, smiling at Pyotr.

"Thank you, Kolya." Pyotr said, taking the note which was only two words:

Pyotr music

"Oh dear!" Pyotr whispered. "Thank you, Kolya. You are indeed a very bright boy."

If only he could hear it, Pyotr would compose a concerto, just for him – something magical, full of wonder and infinite possibilities.

A FEW DAYS LATER PYOTR STILL FELT INSPIRED BY KOLYA. A bright inquisitive lad trapped in a world of silence – a young mind who Modest claimed could feel 'sonic' vibrations, but who could only truly experience the world through his eyes. As he thought about the boy, Pyotr kept hearing a mournful melodic phrase bursting with hope and promise.

"You seem distracted," his host said, as he poured drinks. "But thank you for coming to see me on such short notice."

Pyotr chuckled. "When the director of the Imperial Theatres

of Moscow invites one to share a glass of wine and discuss an *idea*," he smiled, "one makes time. Quickly."

Vladimir Begichev grinned. "Pyotr Ilyich, you are much too formal with someone you've known as long as me."

Begichev handed Pyotr a glass and walked over to the pianoforte dominating the drawing room. "It was in this very room that I introduced you to Mademoiselle Artôt, and watched her cast a spell over you. Remember?"

Pyotr raised an eyebrow. "Please tell me you're not trying to find me a wife again."

Begichev shook his head. "No, Pyotr. I know about your, er... inclinations. My stepson Vladimir has similar ones." Begichev tapped the keys of the pianoforte. "Except he is already a man of considerable financial means, thanks to his inheritance. And now that he is to be married to an even more prosperous family, he will even become a count."

"Count Vladimir Shilovsky?" Pyotr smiled. "And will he find a way to keep his 'inclinations' hidden from his wife?"

Begichev shrugged.

"Is this the 'idea' you wanted to discuss?" Pyotr asked. "That I find a wife who will afford me a title and a stable income?"

"No. I have something much more important," Begichev lifted his glass of wine to his lips. "I am expanding the repertoire at the Bolshoi Theatre." He took a sip. "I want to commission a ballet score from you." Begichev set the glass on top of the polished pianoforte. "If you're interested, of course."

"A ballet?" Pyotr hesitated. "Some light music for a few dances?"

"No, no! I want something grand, something spectacular! Maybe like the operas in Paris. Remember *Guillaume Tell?*"

Pyotr nodded. "Of course. It was... well, it was quite beyond compare." He studied his own glass. "But a ballet is not an opera, there is no singing, no..." the face of young Kolya flashed in his head, "no words."

"Exactly! Only I want *your* music, with the best dancers and most inventive staging we find. Think about it. We will create a feast for the eyes, as much as for the ears." Begichev remained standing at the pianoforte. "I'm searching for a libretto at the moment. Something... something unusual."

Pyotr flushed with excitement. He'd only ever played around with ballet for fun, entertaining his young nieces with a song for them to dance to. They loved it, but maybe this was a chance to do something special. "What about a fantasy?" he asked. "A story perhaps set in medieval times. It could be magical, fantastic... maybe even a little tragic?"

Begichev sat down at the pianoforte. He reached over to the keys furthest to his left, and tapped out the darkest notes. "I have an idea you might like. It's inspired by an old German fairy-tale, or maybe it's Russian, I'm not sure."

"A fairytale? That might work. Which one?"

"*The Lake of Swans*," Begichev smiled. "And I will pay you four times your monthly salary from teaching at the conservatory. I am offering you eight hundred rubles to write music that will turn a fairytale into a work of art."

"Eight hundred?" Pyotr repeated, bowing his head. "I accept, most humbly. Hopefully I will not disappoint you."

EVERYTHING ABOUT LATE JUNE IN THE TINY VILLAGE OF Usovo and the surrounding countryside felt right to Pyotr. It was like returning to an old friend. The meandering streams running to the nearby Moskva River babbled happily, greeting him as if he'd never left.

Since arriving here three weeks ago, visiting the summer estate of Vladimir Shilovsky, Pyotr had settled into a regular routine – one most conducive to finishing the draft of his third symphony.

Each morning he woke early and walked by the stream near the woods to listen and gather inspiration. With the music of nature still playing in his head, he headed back to shower with cool water from the well. After breakfast he spent the rest of the morning drafting ideas for the symphony before meeting Vladimir for their mid-day meal.

Frequently they would end up in the new bathhouse next to the stables. Today they lingered, taking time to enjoy a long steam bath.

"My stepfather is counting on your ballet to make him the most loved man in Moscow," Vladimir smiled as he ladled water onto the steaming rocks. "But what does he know of love?"

Pyotr studied Vladimir standing in all his naked glory, beads of perspiration running down his smooth chest. His rosy lips were wet and full. His matted hair was styled as if each strand's placement had been orchestrated by a talented wigmaker.

Their 'love' was occasional and physical – but it was deep friendship that truly bound them together.

"Your stepfather has a vision. I will not let him down," Pyotr replied, but as Vladimir sat down next to him, his intent was obvious. He touched Pyotr's lips softly, followed by a kiss so tender it was impossible to resist.

Passion overtook them quickly as clouds of steam drifted over them. Their bodies entangled with urgency. Both men glowed in the aftermath of their passion, bodies glistening.

"Is it true?" Pyotr whispered as he lay covered by a towel on the lower bench. "You are to be married, my soul?"

Vladimir laughed. "Ha! You're jealous?"

"No, but I love this place... and after you are married," Pyotr hesitated. Living a lie could crush one's spirit forever. But admitting the truth could be even worse. "I don't know what will happen." He rolled over and whispered into the wooden slats of the bench. "I will not be able to see you."

"You are so dramatic, master!" Vladimir exclaimed. "It's not for another year and besides, I will be a young buck of twenty-five and Anna an old maid – almost thirty-seven!"

He sprang onto the floor, displaying his youthful form proudly. "I will *always* make time for you."

"No," Pyotr replied reaching for his robe. "We must both resist our nature. Perhaps..." an idea was taking shape in his head, "perhaps I will take a bride as well."

Vladimir shook his head. "Music is your only..."

"Listen, my soul," Pyotr cut him off. "I care about how we will be remembered. You must be a true husband for your wife. As I must be for mine."

Though he spoke with conviction, Pyotr's words rang hollow in his mind. He stared at Vladimir beckoning him once more.

Pyotr closed his eyes searching for conviction. "And, when I am married, I will seek treatment and live as a man was meant to live with his wife."

THE APPLAUSE WAS STRONG AND THE AUDIENCE'S ENTHUSIASM should have gladdened Pyotr, but the first public performance of his Third Symphony left him feeling cold. Maybe it was the frigid November weather, but if this was the best he could do, perhaps he needed ...

"Pyotr Ilyich!" a voice broke his thoughts.

Most everyone had left the theatre except for a few players who lingered at the back of the hall. He turned and smiled at the sight of Nikolay Rubinstein who had conducted the performance. He carried a bottle of champagne and three glasses on a tray.

He approached with a lively man at his side, somewhat shorter than Nikolay, with a long narrow nose and heavy eyelids – features that seemed Jewish to Pyotr. The man stepped closer and bowed his head.

"Pyotr Ilyich," Nikolay repeated. "You have a new admirer. I believe someone you yourself appreciate."

Pyotr studied the man; the face was not familiar.

"May I introduce Camille Saint-Saëns from Paris," Nikolay said. "He's giving recitals this week across Moscow."

"Maestro!" Pyotr exclaimed. "Of course I know your work, but I am sorry, I did not know your face. I'm honoured to meet you."

"*Merci,*" Camille replied. "And may I be the first to congratulate you on your new symphony. I very much enjoyed the scherzos."

"I think you're being too generous, sir. There are hardly any new ideas. And I believe I made the first movement too difficult for the orchestra..."

"Nonsense!" Nikolay interrupted. "The players are challenged, but the work shines."

"Agreed," Camille replied. "Don't change a thing." He smiled. "Get better players."

Somehow coming from Camille, an accomplished composer with perfect pitch and innovative ideas, Pyotr felt uplifted. "Thank you." He glanced over at Nikolay still holding the champagne. "Are we going to have a drink or not?"

The men found seats in the front row of the empty theatre. The last of the musicians left and after a second bottle of champagne, the exchange of ideas about music, politics and weather had run its course.

"Is it true that you've taken a young bride, Camille?" Nikolay prodded. "Only nineteen?"

"*Oui, c'est vrai,*" Camille said with a grin. "Just before I turned forty and became too old for her."

Pyotr smiled. "And how do you find married life?"

Camille sighed. "I'm difficult to live with, but Marie-Laure, is, well..." He hesitated, staring at his empty glass. "Some of her talents are quite considerable!"

Nikolay laughed. "And you left your marriage bed to come to Moscow in November?"

"Sometimes the mind requires warmth too," he replied. "But I suppose the perfect woman exists only in Greek legends," he paused looking at Pyotr. "Or perhaps, in magical ballets?"

"Yes, Camille," Nikolay replied. "You've heard Pyotr is working on a ballet? It's about a swan who turns into a beautiful princess at night, and captures the heart of a prince."

Camille rose to his feet. "A swan," he repeated, "woman-hood... in its purest form. That is inspiring!"

He lifted his arms and began imitating a bird taking flight, flapping imaginary wings before lifting both arms gracefully in the air, rising up on his toes and taking an exaggerated bow. "May I audition for a part in your production?"

"Certainly!" Pyotr cried. "But you must try much harder, Camille. Observe."

Pyotr removed his shoes, ran up to the theatre stage and danced across it as gracefully as he could. He imitated Camille's attempts to fly, but added a pirouette, before falling to his knees.

Loud applause from Nikolay and Camille followed. "Pyotr, stay there. I have an idea," Nikolay called out. He took a seat on the piano, still in place on stage from the concert. "Do you two know the story of *Pygmalion and Galatea?*" he called out. "Pygmalion builds the perfect woman, who Aphrodite brings to life. It's a ballet and you two are going to dance it!"

Camille laughed as he joined Pyotr on stage. "Who do I play?" he asked, removing his jacket and shoes.

"Galatea," Nikolay responded. "The most perfect woman ever created, silent and adoring, an angel. Of course, you live only for Pygmalion."

"That's me, I suppose?" Pyotr smiled.

"Yes," Nikolay replied quickly. "I'll play. You two, dance!"

With that, he began to perform the 'ballet' on the piano, an improvisation drawn from Pyotr's music alternating with Camille's concertos. The two men on stage danced as best they could, laughing at each other until they collapsed in a heap as Nikolay reached the dramatic climax to his impromptu orchestration.

As Pyotr lay panting on the stage, hurting from so much laughter, not to mention a twisted ankle and sheer physical exertion, he closed his eyes and felt more at peace than he had in many, many years.

And all at once music came to him – a dance for a white swan... a swan pure of heart, like Camille's young bride in her nuptial bed. And then a dark counterpoint, chords of shame for the temptations of the black swan that haunted lesser men.

Men with desires like his.

———

THE TRAIN PULLED AWAY FROM MOSCOW STATION ON WHAT seemed like the coldest night yet of the long, bone-chilling, nearly exhausted December. Pyotr turned his gaze from the receding platform to watch as young Kolya reached for another fried *pelmeni*. The boy dipped the dumpling into a saucer of sour cream and popped the whole mess into his mouth.

"Mmmmmm" Kolya murmured. His eyes widened. He swallowed hard, and extended his hand toward the almost empty bowl of warm *pelmeni* on the table in their plush sleeping berth.

Pyotr's brother Modest covered the bowl with his hand. "One more," he said holding up the index finger of his other hand. "Okay?"

The boy nodded his head, and as soon as Modest uncovered the bowl, Kolya grabbed the last two dumplings and pushed himself back against the chair, guarding his precious cargo.

Modest pointed to the empty bowl. "No!" he scolded, wagging his finger. "I said *one!*"

"Modi," Pyotr chided his brother. "Let him eat!"

Pyotr made a silly face at Modest. Kolya stuck his tongue out and quickly devoured both dumplings.

Though Pyotr feared his brother would be upset, he only laughed. When the boy was done eating he moved close to Modest and said quietly. "Sorr-eee."

Modest patted his head and smiled.

Pyotr was taken back. "He can talk?"

"Just a few words," Modest replied. The pride in his eyes was clear. "I'm going to teach him more."

"Tell me more about this school in Lyon," Pyotr said. "Are all the students deaf?"

"Yes," Modest replied. "They have a new method of teaching deaf-mutes. That's why I will be spending the whole year there, learning how it works."

"But... is Kolya mute?"

"He is deaf, so it's hard for him to know how to form words." Modest studied the boy a moment. "But he is a sponge – so thirsty for knowledge. He is reading. He is writing, and so eager too."

Modest reached under the table for something in his sack. He laid a slate board and a piece of chalk on the table and wrote a few words on it. He pushed the slate towards Kolya:

Ask Pyotr something

Kolya grabbed the slate. He wiped it clean with his fingers, reached for the chalk and began to slowly write words on it. When he was done, he turned the slate around so Pyotr could read:

Tell me story swan ballet

"Really? You want to know about it?" Pyotr asked. He turned to Modest. "You told him about my ballet?"

"A little. He had so many questions, but I don't know the story."

Pyotr wondered how he could explain the libretto. Since he'd finished his Third Symphony, he had immersed himself in the ballet which Begichev was now calling 'Swan Lake.' As the music took shape, Pyotr was growing more confident in his craftsmanship. Nikolay Rubinstein acclaimed his new symphony and even Mily Balakirev approved.

And then his opera, *Vakoula the Smith,* had won a competition in Petersburg with praise from none other than stern Nikolay Rimsky-Korsakov. Maybe, Pyotr dared dream, just maybe, there would be less music to feed his little stove this year.

Modest poked Pyotr's arm. "Tell him about the ballet. He likes the idea of a lady turning into a swan."

"Yes, yes!" Pyotr exclaimed. "Modi, write this down on the slate."

Pyotr found Kolya's eye. "There was once a beautiful princess named Odette. But she was enchanted by an evil witch. Every day Odette turns into a swan swimming on a lake. Every night she turns back into a beautiful woman."

He paused a moment. "Am I going too fast?"

"Just a minute," Modest replied, writing the last few words on the slate and then taking a sheaf of paper to finish. He pushed both texts over to Kolya who read it slowly then looked up, his mouth gaping open. Pinching the air, he stretched an invisible line between his two hands.

"He wants more," Modest explained.

Pyotr smiled. "When Prince Siegfried finds the lake of swans, he falls in love with Odette. The spell will be broken if he pledges his love to her and marries her. But instead, he is tricked and promises to marry the witch's daughter who is disguised by magic as Odette."

After Modest wrote the words down and Kolya read them, the boy's face tightened. "Happy end?" he wrote on the slate.

Modest glanced at Pyotr. "Do they live happily ever after?"

"Of course not," Pyotr replied. "We are Russian." He bit his lip. "Prince Siegfried and Odette have no choice. Since they cannot be together, they throw themselves into the lake of their tears and are united for eternity in the afterlife."

Kolya gasped after he read the words on the slate, lowered his head and Pyotr could see the boy's eyes were wet. Kolya pulled the slate toward him, erased the words with his hand and began to write. When he was done, he turned the slate around to show Pyotr:

Want to see your ballet

———————

TWO WEEKS LATER IT WAS PYOTR'S TURN TO AWAIT SOMEONE else's performance. As the lights in the Paris theatre opera house dimmed, he held his breath. Tonight, he would finally get to experience the magic of *Carmen* for himself.

Vladimir Shilovsky had been lucky enough to see the premiere here in March and sent a copy of the score to Pyotr shortly afterwards. The music carried Pyotr away. No other modern composition had ever touched him like this. When he learned the composer, George Bizet, died of a sudden heart attack after the opera's thirty-third performance, Pyotr found himself filled with a terrible sadness at losing such a gifted musical colleague.

But now, Bizet was alive again, his voice ready to fill the hushed opera house. Pyotr glanced at his brother, Modi, as transfixed by the rising curtain as he.

A bell rang out from the orchestra. Cigarette girls and urchin boys emerged on stage, dressed in the clothing of the proletariat. Sweat and dirt from their jobs covered them as they engaged in idle banter. A young woman sauntered on stage – confidently provocative, wildly alluring – obviously the star of the show.

Carmen.

Pyotr leaned closer to the stage. The woman held every eye with her commanding presence, although she had yet to utter a sound. Preening soldiers surrounded her, each wanting to get closer. One man asked when she would decide who is most worthy. Who would be the one lucky enough to win her heart?

Carmen lowered her head as the opening four note tango

rhythm of the first aria, 'Habanera,' slowly began to resonate through the opera house. Pyotr sat mesmerized. The cellos established the melody – darkly Spanish and hypnotically simple, until the mezzo-soprano star of the show, Célestine Galli-Marié began to growl:

> *L'amour est un oiseau rebelle*
> *Que nul ne peut apprivoiser*
> *Et c'est bien en vain qu'on l'appelle*
> *S'il lui convient de refuser*

A chill shivered down Pyotr's neck. His head tingled.

Célestine's voice was powerful and sultry, almost wickedly so. Dressed as a peasant girl with mounds of dishevelled black hair and darting wild eyes, she sang in a most provocative manner. Her untamed passion poured from the stage, holding Pyotr in her grasp.

"She's wonderful!" Pyotr whispered, turning toward his brother.

"Yes... is she ever!" Modest replied without taking his eyes from her.

As the opera continued, Pyotr could not remember ever being so captivated. On paper, the score had delighted him. But it was no match for seeing it live. It was like reading a recipe for cooked chicken compared to tasting a brandied *coq au vin*.

With such piquant orchestration, a brilliantly decorated stage, talented performers with split-second timing and the shining star in the middle – Célestine Galli-Marié as Carmen, Pyotr felt truly humbled.

Could he ever match such a wonder as this?

MOSCOW, MAY 1876 *(AGE 36)*

. . .

"I CAN'T DANCE TO THIS," THE GREY-EYED BRUNETTE PLAYING
the Swan Princess repeated for the second time as she stopped
dancing yet again. "It's not even a ballet. It's a very... very, *boring*
symphony."

Pyotr sank lower in his seat a dozen rows back from the
Bolshoi's theatre stage.

"Lydia, my dearest. Not to worry," the ballet master, Julius
Reisinger crooned. "We can change the music. It's not that
important anyway." He rushed towards her as if to save her from
imminent danger. "What would you like for your *pas de deux?*"

The scene unfolding on stage before Pyotr this morning was
only the latest insult. Since finishing his *Swan Lake* commission
in April, for which he had yet to be fully paid, he had endured
over a month of painful rehearsals in which his role was reduced
to curious spectator. And he was told this morning the
remaining money owed to him would be taken from performance receipts and paid out over time.

"No, Julius, that's not enough to save this mess," the troubled
Swan Princess, Lydia Geiten, announced standing up on her toes
for a second, before sinking down flat-footed. "I can't do it." She
sighed loudly. "I quit."

She walked from the stage, head held high in disdain as she
shot a stinging glance toward Pyotr before disappearing behind
the curtain.

He watched her leave with a mixture of regret and relief.
Though he'd laboured over the ballet these past nine months, it
seems he'd not understood what it took to compose a ballet. But
at least the difficult-to-please Swan Princess was gone.

"She's right you know!" Julius, the ballet master shouted at
him from the stage. Pyotr shook his head in dismay. Despite
numerous requests to clarify the requirements for the ballet, the
moody Czech who was choreographing the production never
bothered to provide Pyotr with any guidance whatsoever.

Julius waved to him. "Bring me your score!"

Up on stage, Pyotr watched as Julius flipped through the

pages. "Nope! Nope! Nope..." He mumbled, tearing off corners of various pages. "The music for these scenes is unsuitable for ballet. Remove them."

"But, they are necessary, to build the motif, the theme. You can't just..." Pyotr's objections were met with a raised hand.

"No one cares," Julius snapped, "no one will remember it anyway. The music is just to give the dancers tempo and rhythm. Every music specialist knows that." His voice was laced with anger. "I just hope Anna will dance to..." he shoved the score back at Pyotr, "whatever this is supposed to be."

Pyotr burned.

Yes, he had rejected the simple approach to scoring ballet music in favour of something that would marry two art forms. He had written thirty-one different compositions including the *leitmotiv* of the ballet, the 'Swan Theme' with images of the dancers being carried away by the melody.

He must have taken leave of his senses. How could he have been so wrong?

"Anna," Julius called out to one of the ballerinas off to the side of the stage. "The lead is yours now... if you want it."

Tiny Anna Sobeshchanskaya rushed to Julius, touched his arm and whispered something. She ignored Pyotr completely. He turned and headed back to his seat. Julius shuffled off the stage, had brief words with the conductor and then gave a sign to Anna and the only male dancer on the stage, Victor Gillert.

The music began and Anna and Victor began their *pas de deux*. But something was wrong. This wasn't the music Pyotr had composed. It was... wait. What was it?

Pyotr was furious. He strode towards Julius standing beside the conductor. "Stop!" Pyotr shouted. "What is this?"

"Minkus," Julius replied nonchalantly. "Ludwig Minkus." He smirked at Pyotr. "Anna said she would take the lead, but she wants this music for her *pas de deux*. And it's her decision, so..."

"Whether this ballet is good or bad, I alone am responsible for its music," Pyotr shouted. He glanced at the sheet music on the conductor's podium. He softened his tone. "I will create a new *pas de deux* for Anna, to her exact specifications if required."

"Fine," Julius retorted. "But whether the ballet is good or bad, it will be *me* they remember. It's not the music that will define *Swan Lake*."

FINALLY, THE DAY HAD ARRIVED – FRIDAY, THE FOURTH OF March, eighteen seventy-seven – the premiere of *Swan Lake* at the Bolshoi Theatre in Moscow.

Pyotr had endured countless revisions and created a new *pas de deux* for Anna, preserving the exact lengths and divisions of an arrangement by Ludwig Minkus. And although she thought Pyotr's composition superior, Anna was gone. There were hushed rumours she was fired by the Governor General of Moscow who she agreed to marry before running off with another dancer and keeping the Governor General's jewels.

But none of that mattered now. What started as a curious musical challenge had evolved into a full and very innovative symphonic score. Was it too much for an audience that preferred light melodies with their ballets and caviar? He had built it around themes that developed throughout the ballet, building them in waves of emotion that he hoped would fuse the music to the choreography and the staging. He was most proud of how the oboe solo for Odette and her swans had come together during the last few rehearsals.

The curtain rose as the overture finished. Pyotr held his breath. Beside him sat Karl Valts, the stage designer of the production. He leaned over as the music began. "Your music," he whispered, "it lives here." He touched his chest.

Pyotr nodded politely, but kind words couldn't quell his growing fear.

The ballet began outside of Prince Siegfried's castle and

proceeded smoothly until finally Polina Karpakova, in the role of Odette, fluttered out from the side of the stage. The dance of the swans soon followed with Victor Gillert dancing as the Prince. The music and dances worked together, just as Pyotr had intended, with the conductor coaxing out moments of magical orchestration, staying true to the different tonalities Pyotr intended.

But as the curtain came down on Act I and the dark tones foreshadowing Act II faded, Pyotr heard voices behind him.

"What in the world was that?" a man asked harshly.

"Is this whole thing German?" a woman replied. "What a stupid story!"

Pyotr wanted to turn and face his critics, but instead sat motionless, his face flushed, waiting for the second act. As it started, his mind fretted about the final storm scene. Karl, the stage designer was gone, probably to supervise the effect of the lake bursting its banks, flooding the stage with hundreds of pails of water.

Somehow Karl made it look like a real whirlpool, branches and boughs falling into the water and being swept away. When the production was finally finished, and the curtain lowered, Pyotr sat breathing heavily, sweat rolling down his forehead, his shirt soaked.

He looked over at the Karl's empty seat and imagined young Kolya sitting there. Would his face be full of joy and wonder at the spectacle that had just transpired on stage? Or perhaps he too would be disappointed, like the disparaging couple seated behind him who hissed as they rose to their feet to leave, "Thank the Lord that's over!"

Pyotr had been a midwife at the birth of something quite new. But would it be a shunned creature, forever despised and unloved?

The polite applause quickly died down and within a few days the critics savaged the production. "It was far too complicated for a ballet," they wrote. "The music was too noisy, too

Wagnerian and too symphonic. The choreography was unimaginative and altogether unmemorable."

To add insult, Pyotr collected only one hundred rubles from the premiere, of the five hundred still owed to him. The lead dancer, Polina, meanwhile collected almost two thousand rubles, half the opening night box-office.

Pyotr had invested much of his emotional and creative energies for nearly two years on *Swan Lake,* only to have it ridiculed. And now he would be lucky to ever collect the rest of his measly eight hundred rubles.

To top it off, he was feverish and afflicted with constant attacks of catarrh. He would take his doctor's advice and leave Russia, maybe to Vichy in France to take the waters and forget about working on another ballet ever again.

CHAPTER 10

"We can change the music. It's not that important anyway". With these words, Reisinger perfectly summarizes the role of music in 19th century ballet. It might seem a strange notion today to anyone who has frequented the ballet and experienced the marriage of music and dance firsthand, but our modern views on ballet are significantly different to those of Tchaikovsky's time.

Ballet traces its origin back to the 15th century. In the Italian courts of those days, it was a form of entertainment in which nobles took an active part. A dancing master would teach the steps to the assembled gentry, and the guests then participated in a large performance. Professional dancers played supporting roles, but the dance itself took center stage.

These ballets flourished in the French courts as well in the centuries to follow. Louis XIV, the Sun King, who was considered a gifted dancer himself, was responsible for establishing two academies that would fuel the evolution of ballet further, even when the performances themselves faded from the courts. Ballet as an artform blossomed, with dance and performance being the key elements. The music was just there to support the dance.

When Tchaikovsky accepted the commission for Swan

Lake, he had little experience with composing for ballet, and as a result he was not hindered by how things had always been done. He approached the matter as a symphonic composer, meaning he devoted considerable time to the progression of thematic material, much more than was common in music for ballet at the time. As Reisinger's words illustrate, music merely served as a backdrop for the dancers, and if the music was not suitable, it was replaced. Ballet music was often light, and clear in rhythm, facilitating the dancer's movements. The music that Tchaikovsky wrote for Swan Lake, however, was much more complex. The music developed slowly throughout, growing into symphonic proportions, and had a heavier sense of drama than was expected in music for ballet. Tchaikovsky had succeeded in writing an elaborate symphonic piece with a strong narrative supported by musical techniques. Quite the accomplishment.

Though the music for Swan Lake was groundbreaking and original, its choreographer Reisinger did not give it the treatment that it deserved. Instead of seizing upon the opportunity to create a next level of choreography that would take advantage of the musical possibilities, he dismissed various parts of the score as impossible to use. His approach to Swan Lake was a traditional one in the ballet world; the music was mostly irrelevant, there to keep the beat and set the mood. Anything that was deemed too complex was replaced or dropped. Reisinger even introduced music from other composers, clearly showing how little he thought of the role of musical composition.

It was not surprising that Reisinger took this approach with Swan Lake. A few exceptions withstanding, most ballet music was written to order: music was composed to suit the dance and timing on stage. A composer might be called upon to add sixteen bars of a certain dance or rhythmic type to facilitate a transition, and music could be added and discarded at the whim of the ballet master. Because of this, ballet music could easily resemble a patchwork of loosely threaded musical pieces, merely existing to tie the previous dance to the next one. This had a severe impact on the coherence of the music.

TCHAIKOVSKY HOWEVER APPROACHED SWAN LAKE AS A symphonic composer, meaning he worked within a clear, larger structure, tying musical elements together with motives, consistency of instrumentation and harmony, and plenty of room for musical development to support this larger structure. In symphonic works, musical ideas evolve more slowly and elaborately, guiding the listener through each phase. Instead of a collection of short anecdotes that might differ in style, color, and grammar, he created a large-scale musical narrative that takes the entire duration of the performance to unfold.

As a result, Swan Lake gives much more attention to the music itself than was common in ballet at that time, with various longer instrumental sections that exist to give proper time and space for musical ideas, as is common in symphonic music.

This is not to say that all ballet music until Swan Lake was merely a hodgepodge of musical ditties. Composers such as Pugni, Minkus and Delibes wrote exquisite music for dance, featuring highly melodious and intricate numbers. The more Tchaikovsky studied their works, the more he became impressed by the highly skilled variations and melodies they had written.

Nevertheless, the difference between Swan Lake and most ballet music up until then was enormous. With much more intricate and longer musical build-up throughout the work, heavier instrumentation, complex harmonic structures, and the usage of other tools he employed as a symphonic composer, Swan Lake could not possibly be compared to conventional ballet music at the time.

It may not be entirely surprising that the première of Swan Lake was not well received. Ballet audiences were not prepared for this type of work, and many spectators and critics considered the music much too complex and too grand for ballet. Combined with Reisinger's conventional choreography that failed to maximize the opportunities presented by Tchaikovsky's score, and a somewhat meagre production in terms of costumes and décor, Swan Lake was not off to a good start.

In the years to come, various musical and choreographic components of Swan Lake were altered, leading to the version presented all over the world today. Even though Swan Lake is now heralded as a milestone and turning point in the world of ballet, it took a long time from its première to arrive at the recognition it so richly deserved. Unfortunately, the chances of attending a performance of Swan Lake in its original form as composed by Tchaikovsky are more than a bit slim.

The number of changes made over the years, especially after Tchaikovsky's death, and the lack of a complete original score by Tchaikovsky's hand, make it impossible to experience the work as its author originally intended. Nevertheless, with the completion of Swan Lake, Tchaikovsky had unknowingly set in motion a ripple of change throughout the world of ballet that is still tangible in today's performances, proving once and for all that the music, despite Reisinger's claims, mattered very, very much.

CHAPTER 11

MOSCOW, 18 JULY 1877 (AGE 37)

The small group crowding around the table at the Hermitage Restaurant provided meagre comfort to Pyotr on what should have been one of the happiest days of his life.

His wedding day.

"My brother, Pyotr Ilyich, is indeed a very lucky man," Anatoly Tchaikovsky proclaimed raising his glass in a toast to the bride and groom. "His new wife is the heroine of his own little opera, as in love with him as a cat! And as the hero of his own tale, I am quite sure he will not be so cruel as to run and hide from such affection."

Pyotr grimaced at the subtle reference to the libretto of his new opera, *Yevgeny Onegin*. It was no secret that Tolya, as he called Modest's twin, found the idea of Pyotr getting married absurd. But as the only family member able to attend the last minute wedding, his blessing would have to suffice.

"A toast then, to my big brother and his bride, my new big *sister* Antonina. May she keep her claws sharp." Tolya smiled, extending his flute of champagne across the table to the little wedding party of seven guests – all men except the twenty-eight year old bride, Antonina Miliukova.

Tolya and all the men save Pyotr, held their glasses up high. *"Za-Molodykh!* To the newlyweds!" they sang out.

Everyone took a sip, including the eager bride Antonina. All the men winced in exaggerated protest, indicating the wine was too bitter.

"Gor'ko!" they laughed. *"Gor'ko!"*

Oh lord, Pyotr cursed silently.

He'd forgotten about this stupid tradition. The only way to shut them up, to 'sweeten the wine,' was to kiss the bride. Could no one accept his marriage would be only as a *friend* to Antonina? Yes, he would be a kindly brother for this woman who was in no way repugnant to him, but hardly a suitable lover.

Why could he not just be a husband like so many others? One more man who was not in love with his wife?

He looked over at Iosif Kotek, his brilliant student, a violinist and until a few months ago, Pyotr's most hopeless crush.

"Gor'ko!" all the men, including Iosif, repeated incessantly.

Antonina jumped to her feet and yanked Pyotr up beside her. To loud cheers, she pulled his face to hers and pressed her wet lips to his with an embarrassing display of unbridled lustfulness. He froze, closed his eyes and endured the invasion of his privacy to the laughing catcalls of the other men.

As their train prepared to depart for Petersburg a few hours later, Pyotr sat in silent agony across from his bride. They were alone in their private carriage and he was ready to scream from the sobs that were suffocating him.

"What shall I call you, husband?" Antonina asked gently. *"Peti* or maybe, *Petya?"*

She batted her eyes and pursed her lips. Pyotr acknowledged drily to himself that she was an attractive woman, even if the same compliment could not be paid to her intellect.

He cleared his throat. "My dear, do you understand that we are…" he hesitated, choosing his words carefully, "husband and wife, only in the sense that Plato himself would admire? My desires are more… well, more like that of a dove – a bird who seeks to flock with others of the same feather."

"*Petya!*" she smiled. "You don't have to talk to me like a child. I have loved you since I first laid eyes upon your beautiful face when I was your student at the conservatory. You are the most perfect man I've ever known, with the kindest eyes that ever looked upon me."

She reached across the space between them and touched his knee. "I have even started sewing shirts for you, shirts that will fit you like the man of royalty you will always be to me."

He nodded, unsure how to respond. It was not his nature to be rude or to want to fight.

Antonina leaned back in her chair. "Our wedding was so special for me, *Petya*. Both at the church and then at the dinner. And now that we're off on our honeymoon, I have something special planned for you tonight. Our first night together as man and wife."

Was she daft?

Did she not understand his plain talk about not wanting to be a husband in her bed? He didn't try to respond to her statement, and she happily babbled on, not noticing that he said only enough to be polite. Finally, just after the train began to roll away after a brief station stop at Klin, a life-saving friend burst into the compartment.

"Ah, here you are! Congratulations!" he beamed. "Madam Tchaikovsky, it is an honour to finally meet you. I'm so sorry I was unable to attend the wedding." He bowed his head. "Nikolay Rubinstein, at your service."

Antonina rose and embraced him. "Thank you," she smiled. "Would you care to join us?"

Pyotr bolted up from his chair. "My dear, let me help Nikolay get settled. You stay here and..." he noticed the bag of fabric beside her, "...finish your sewing."

Nikolay began to protest. "Pyotr, it's okay! You stay with your wife, I can..."

"Nonsense, I'm glad to help you!"

With that Pyotr dashed from the sleeping berth, eager to taste the sweet air of freedom. He walked quickly, hurrying towards the next carriage. Nikolay was close behind, and bade him continue through two more carriages until they arrived at his private berth.

Pyotr gave vent to a flood of tears before he could say a word to Nikolay. "I can't do it! I thought it would be so easy, but... I just want to be alone. How did I make such a terrible mistake?"

Nikolay offered him a shot of vodka. "Don't worry my friend. I'll find you your own compartment. I will tell your wife you are unwell. I'm sure she will be fine for one night."

Nikolay left, leaving Pyotr sitting alone. He extinguished the small lamps in the berth and sat still in the darkness in a state of moral torment. The repetitive clacking of the train's steel wheels under his feet as the carriages rolled down the track, provided the only comfort he'd had on this long, miserable day.

Pyotr closed his eyes and folded his hands together.

How had he let this happen?

NINE MONTHS EARLIER...

PYOTR STOOD WAITING FOR THE CARRIAGE HE HAD HIRED ON A frigid moonlit evening in early January. Beside him, Iosif Kotek shivered in the cold, holding his violin case and the sheet music Pyotr had written for him.

Hearing Iosif play the waltz for the first time that day had brought tears of joy to Pyotr. His former student reincarnated the piece into a virtuoso performance of flesh and blood. For years Pyotr had watched this young man develop his musical talents and without realizing it until a few weeks earlier, let him slip deep into his heart.

"I have a confession," Pyotr whispered as the clip-clop of horses grew louder. The carriage taking them to Yar for supper pulled up in front of them, steam from the animals rising in clouds in the crisp winter air.

Iosif waited until they were both comfortably seated inside the coach before he responded. "A confession, maestro?" he asked, his voice stilted from the cold.

"When you came to me with this new commission, this violin concerto for your employer, I realized that for all these years..." Pyotr hesitated, staring at Iosif. "How many since we first met?"

"Six... when I started in your composition class," he looked away, "the same year that Madam Artôt engaged me in her treachery. You remember that night I came to your house?"

"How could I forget?" Pyotr smiled. "Her *treachery* brought you to me that evening. And probably saved me."

Iosif nodded. "I was not aware of her plan and did not mean to..."

"You did nothing wrong," Pyotr interrupted, "and everything right." How could he explain the feelings overflowing within him? "It made me admire you a little bit, and then over the years, more and more each time we were together."

The carriage lurched as they rounded a corner. Iosif was still trembling from the frigid night air. He touched his frosty nose and then tried to cover his ears, which had turned a painful looking shade of crimson. "I'm so cold," he shivered, "I think even my bones are frozen."

Pyotr shuffled from his side of the coach, moving beside Iosif. He took the collar of Iosif's fur coat, wrapping it over his face. Though his own bare hands were freezing, Pyotr felt pleasure with the comfort he was providing.

"Thank you," Iosif smiled. "You are so kind to me."

There was a woollen blanket under the bench Pyotr had been sitting on. He bent over, grabbed it and covered them both. The feeling of intimacy being wrapped so close together was divine.

"What is your confession, maestro?" Iosif asked as Pyotr rubbed his hands together under the blanket trying to warm them.

"Call me, *Petya*. If you..." Pyotr said in an uncertain voice. "But, only if you..."

"*Petya*. I like the way that sounds on my lips," Iosif interrupted, touching Pyotr's hand under the blanket and squeezing it gently. "Now tell me your secret, please."

Pyotr turned toward him, their faces inches apart. "I beg you not to be angry with me, but it is impossible to hide my feelings any longer. I am impossibly in love with you."

The confession brought silence. Only the rhythm of the horses' hooves, clip-clopping in steady 2/4 time, broke the quiet.

Though he said nothing in response, Iosif moved a little closer and laid his head down on Pyotr's chest. It was one of the most intimate feelings Pyotr could recall. Though completely innocent, it filled him with an uncontainable passion.

But it was not physical consummation he needed most. In fact, he would feel only disgust if he gave into his physical desires – an aged, fat-bellied man in his thirties with a unblemished youth of only twenty-two.

It would be horrible. It would ruin everything.

"My heart is yours completely, *kotik*," Pyotr whispered.

Iosif sighed and squeezed Pyotr's hand even tighter under the blanket.

A WEEK LATER, LATE ONE SATURDAY NIGHT, PYOTR SAT AT HIS dining table with his old friends Nikolay Rubinstein who had arrived with wine and vodka, and Vladimir Shilovsky who had arrived with beer and vodka.

The long dark Russian winter held them firmly in its grasp. Outside Pyotr's flat, the windows were thickly frosted in ice and the wind whined mercilessly. Inside, flowing liquor kept the conversation heated and just as pitiless.

"Russians are so lazy!" Pyotr proclaimed, holding a shot of vodka in one hand, and a stein of dark beer in the other. "They like to procrastinate."

"*Da!*" Vladimir growled. "But they don't all procrastinate." He emptied his shot of vodka then reached for his beer. "Some just urinate!"

At this Nikolay raised his glass of wine. "A toast... to urination!"

They all took a long drink and though the mood had gotten silly, Pyotr had more serious matters on his mind. "Gentlemen, I am living a double life you know."

Vladimir sprayed a mouthful of beer out at this statement. "Double life? What, as a man *and* as a peacock?"

"Why not just live as a peacock?" Nikolay laughed. "Take as many roosters as you want, we will never tell." He reached across the table and poured them all more vodka. "To Pyotr! The finest peacock in all of Russia!"

Though a little annoyed, Pyotr drank his vodka shot then set the glass down on the table like a heavy gavel. "Not man and peacock. Man and *artist*."

"Pyotr, Pyotr. Please!" Nikolay growled. "You are an artist and *only* an artist. The other parts of you do not matter. Do whatever you please in your everyday life. But in your 'art-life' you fly with the wings of immortality."

Pyotr snorted. "My wings are broken. I am achieving astonishingly little other than a ripe old age... as a pauper."

Vladimir stood up from the table, opening his leather billfold. "Pyotr, dance with me and I will bestow a hundred rubles upon your wings," he laid a bill on the table, "and fifty kopecks."

He reached into his pocket and laid five coins on top of the paper note.

Shaking his head, Pyotr felt ashamed. Some days his soul throbbed to compose, throbbed with an almost incomprehensible and indescribable excitement. Yet, he still had to live in the everyday world of rent and food and dozens of equally mundane concerns.

He grabbed the money. "You know this is more than I make in a week teaching at the conservatory? More than I make most months from performances of my music?"

Nikolay and Vladimir were silent. The gaiety of the evening had turned sour. Vladimir sat back down. "But isn't *Swan Lake* opening soon? Won't you..."

"It won't bring much," Pyotr interjected. "A ballet with the finest music I could wrench out of my pen, and I'll be lucky to collect a few hundred rubles. And that's only if Reisinger doesn't replace all my music."

"The ballet master is a fool," Nikolay replied. "I'm conducting the orchestra for *Swan Lake*. The musicians revere it." He stared at his empty glass. "As do I. The music stays with me long into the night."

There was more silence. Had Pyotr invited his friends to his house just to console him? Was he grovelling for praise, forcing them to listen to his petty complaints all night long? "Enough weeping, gentlemen. Vladimir, I took your money, now I must dance to fulfill your generous commission."

"Indeed, you must," Vladimir laughed. "Come to me, my beautiful peacock!"

With Nikolay playing a waltz on the piano, Pyotr and Vladimir danced together, and soon the room echoed with laughter again. They kept at it for another hour, with Pyotr taking his turn at the piano to play street music and folk tunes that forced Vladimir and Nikolay to liven their steps.

Much later, as they finally made their goodbyes, Pyotr's heart felt a few pounds lighter. "Thank you, both of you, for listening to my tales of woe."

Vladimir stood at the door, holding his mottled grey rabbit fur *ushanka*. He put the cap on his head and embraced Pyotr tightly. "Perhaps, master, you need to find a wife with means to support your talent."

Pyotr laughed. "After you're married this summer, tell me how that works out for you." He kissed Vladimir softly on the lips. "And for her, given your 'weaknesses'."

Vladimir pulled down the ear flaps of his *ushanka*. "Be always true to yourself, my friend. And if you find the right wife, she will understand."

THE MONTH OF JANUARY EIGHTEEN SEVENTY-SEVEN SEEMED TO go on forever. Some days it was so bitter Pyotr struggled to find enthusiasm to even rise from his bed to brew a cup of tea. Thirty-one days seemed more like thirty-one years.

But still, he was beginning to develop a degree of discipline that might help conquer his shortcomings. As he explained to his friends, he had both an everyday human life and an artistic life. While one brought heaping mounds of anguish, the other delivered a bounty of possibilities to express his emotions – whether sad or joyful, humiliated or exhilarated.

But he could not simply wait for an idea to strike him, or for God, who might suddenly awake in a generous mood, to throw him a musical bone.

"Inspiration is a guest who does not care to visit those who are indolent," he wrote to his brothers Modest and Anatoly. "I compose either from an inward impulse, winged by a lofty and inde-finable inspiration, or I simply *work*, invoking all my powers, which sometimes answer and sometimes remain deaf to my invocation."

Lately, true inspiration was an infrequent, capricious guest.

And yet regardless of what he was doing, or which conversation he was having during the day, that department of his brain devoted to music continued in its useful course. When he later sat down to sketch out a musical idea, he could harvest material that had been germinating within him.

It was exhausting, arduous work nonetheless. It left him drained. And yet to *not* devote himself to composing was unthinkable.

This morning he sat at his writing table, pen in hand, humming a single bar. It was for his new composition in C Major for solo violin and orchestra, the *Valse-Scherzo*. It was for Iosif, the young man who held Pyotr's heart completely. He had requested the music on behalf of his mysterious employer.

There was a knock on the door and before he could rise from his chair, Iosif let himself in and stood in his fur coat and ushanka, shaking snow from his collar. "I'm sorry for barging in, but I have a letter for you."

Pyotr took Iosif's coat and cap and stood in the entryway basking in the warmth of this unexpected visit. "Come in, come in, *kotik*. I just made tea."

Iosif smiled. His face shone with the rosy glow of the winter air, and after tea was poured Pyotr opened Iosif's envelope.

"She can't stop talking about you," Iosif said, taking another sip of tea. "I think she knows every piece of music you've ever composed. Always she asks me and the others in our little troupe to begin with 'Tchaikovsky' even before Beethoven or Mozart!"

Pyotr smiled as he opened the envelope. He gasped when he saw what was inside: a banknote for one thousand rubles and a perfumed letter in a refined hand:

"Honoured Sir,

Allow me to express my sincere thanks for the prompt execution of my commission.

I deem it superfluous to tell you of the enthusiasm I feel for your music, because you are doubtless accustomed to receiving homage of a very different kind to any which could be offered you by so insignificant a person, musically speaking, as myself. It might, therefore, seem ridiculous to you; and my admiration is something so precious that I do not care to have it laughed at.

Therefore I will only say one thing, which I beg you to accept as the literal truth—that your music makes life easier and pleasanter to live."

The signature was neat and clear: *Nadezhda F. von Meck.*

"This must be a mistake," Pyotr whistled. "One thousand rubles for a few sheets of music?"

"*Nyet,*" Iosif replied. "I told her you had," he coughed nervously, "well... debts."

Pyotr laid the banknote on the table. He stared at it, then bit his hand. "But this is too much, what does she..."

"Music, *Petya,*" Iosif said softly. "She wants to commission more music from you, a funeral march." He hesitated, "but she is unsure if you will accept." He walked over to where his coat had been hung and reached into the breast pocket. "This is the other letter I was asked to give you, but only if you will consider such a commission."

"This woman, Nadezhda, by what means does she..."

"Her husband Karl von Meck died last year," Iosif interrupted, "and left her a very rich widow from building all those train tracks. She is smart and knows more about music, literature and science than any woman I've ever met. Or any man for that matter. She even speaks four languages."

Pyotr felt anxious. There must be a catch. "Should I meet with her?"

"I'm not sure, but she talks about you endlessly."

Pyotr hesitated. A funeral march? Hadn't such a commission done in *Herr* Mozart? With some trepidation, he nodded. "Yes, I accept."

"Good," Iosif approached and handed him the folded note.

"Dear Sir—Pyotr Ilyich.

I do not know how to express my thanks for your kind indulgence for my impatience. Were it not for the real sympathy I feel for you, I should be afraid you might want to get rid of me; but I value your kindness too greatly for this to happen.

I should like to tell you a great deal about my fantastic feelings towards you, but I am afraid of taking up your leisure, of which you have so little to spare. I will only say that this feeling —abstract as it may be—is one of the best and loftiest emotions ever yet experienced by any human being. Therefore you may call me eccentric, or mad, if you please; but you must not laugh at me. All this would be ridiculous, if it were not so sincere and serious.

There is one particular number in your *Oprichnik* about which I am wildly enthusiastic. If it is possible, please arrange this for me as a funeral march for four hands (pianoforte). I am sending you the opera in which I have marked the passages I should like you to arrange. If my request is tiresome, do not hesitate to refuse; I shall be regretful, but not offended.

Furthermore, allow me in future to drop all formalities of 'Dear Sir,' etc., in my letters to you; they are not in my style, and I shall be glad if you will write to me without any of this conventional politeness. You will not refuse me this favour?

Yours, with devotion and respect, N. F."

Pyotr was overwhelmed, but also a little confused. "What does the 'F'' stand for?" Pyotr asked, showing the letter to Iosif who quickly read it.

"Filaretovna," Iosif replied. He looked up at Pyotr. "It seems you have captured her heart."

"But my heart belongs only to you, *kotik.*"

At this Iosif looked away. "I have a girlfriend, but I will leave her, if you want to be with me... in that way."

NAKED UNDER HIS SHEETS, PYOTR CLOSED HIS EYES AND wondered. Could life finally be everything he had ever dared hope it could be?

Was he finally emotionally sober?

The warm tendrils of April were beginning to kiss the long Moscow winter *adieu.* Though the critics despised *Swan Lake* which opened last month, and he had yet to collect the remaining three hundred rubles owed to him, the production continued to run at the Bolshoi.

Meanwhile, Nikolay had brought the house down with his inspired conducting of Pyotr's symphonic fantasia, *Francesca da Rimini,* which premiered not three weeks ago. Moscow's warm reception to the work was gratifying.

And now his new violin concerto *Valse-Scherzo* was finished, and once published in Berlin he would unveil it to the world. Experiencing Iosif's virtuoso performance of the first section, with his perfect delicate fingers coaxing each sacred vibration from his strings, was more precious to Pyotr than if it was being performed across the capitals of Europe.

And with the concerto complete, he could fully engross himself in a new work, his Symphony No. 4 in F Minor. Though only in sketch form at this point in his small copy book, the first movement, *Andante sostenuto,* was already teasing him with delicious promise.

He rolled over, glancing at the single candle burning brightly on the nightstand. Where was *kotik,* his little tomcat? Iosif had promised to come by after his rehearsals and spend the night. Last week they had finally consummated their love. A night of tender moments followed by a river of joyful tears.

An hour later, Pyotr was beginning to fret. He was growing sleepy and finally after another forty minutes he could no longer remain in bed waiting. Wrapping himself in his robe, he padded over to the window. Could the rumours about Iosif be true?

Had he not left his girlfriend?

The thought of him with her, Eybozhenko, a former class-mate from the conservatory, filled Pyotr with rage – torture he would rather push away, lest it ruin the contentment of the past few days.

No, he told himself, it could not be. "He is my *kotik*. I am in his heart."

An hour later Pyotr finally heard the door to his flat open. The thick candle burned low, as he waited anxiously to be with Iosif once again, wrapped together in a communion of unholy ecstasy.

"*Kotik?*" he whispered as footsteps approached. A shadow grew closer. It was him, finally! Iosif sat down on the edge of the bed.

"What happened?" Pyotr asked. "I've been waiting for you, my love."

"Sorry," Iosif replied. The smell of vodka filled the room. "I had... a mishap."

Pyotr grabbed the sheet and sat up, suddenly feeling foolish in his nakedness. "A mishap? What happened?"

Iosif shuffled closer on the bed. He held up his left hand. His index finger was wrapped in a bloodied cloth. "I broke my finger and I need something... for the pain."

Pyotr sprang from the bed, found his robe and returned with antiseptic spirit. He sat down beside Iosif. "Let me see."

Gingerly, Iosif unwrapped the bandage. Pyotr gasped at the bloodied, crushed finger. A cracked fingernail protruded hideously over raw flesh. "My God! What have you done?"

Pyotr dabbed the finger with the pungent spirit. Iosif shrieked in pain and recoiled. "I'm so stupid. I was drunk... when she did this."

"Who?"

Iosif cursed, still flinching from the antiseptic. "Eybozhenko. I shouldn't have told her about you." He groaned again as Pyotr applied more of the spirit to the open gash.

"What did she do?"

"Kicked me out, and when I tried to get back into her room, slammed the door on my finger." He held his finger up and Pyotr couldn't avert his eyes from bloodied finger, the same one that coaxed magic from Iosif's violin.

"So it's true then," Pyotr hissed darkly. "You and her... are lovers?"

Iosif hung his head. The candle on the nightstand flickered, casting dark shadows. "Yes," he finally murmured.

"You were with her all night?"

"Yes, I'm sorry. And all day too."

The rage inside Pyotr exploded. "You lying snake!" He was shaking with the thought of them together, having sex and worse... making love. "Do you love her?"

"No, of course not!"

She'd ruined him and stolen something sacred. She used her hymen to corrupt Iosif and if that wasn't enough, castrate the part of him that made music. "How many times?" he screamed. "How many times did you fuck her yesterday?"

"Please, no! Don't talk like..."

"How many?" Pyotr bellowed. "Tell me!"

"I'm not sure, maybe five or six..."

"Get out! Get out of my sight! And take your..." Pyotr could see only red, "your bloody mess straight to hell. Go take it to your whore!"

THE WARMING RAYS OF THE JUNE SUN COULD NOT THAW Pyotr's frozen core. Gone were any traces of gaiety. There was no fun left within him. Life was wearisome. Trivial. Empty.

He cursed the tall pink rose bush bursting with joy at the corner of Tverskaya Street and Maly Gnezdnikovsky Lane. "Bah!" he hissed at their naiveté in revealing themselves so unabashedly.

He felt inside his jacket again for the letter from Antonina Ivanovna Miliukova, a former student he had no recollection of whatsoever. "I have loved you with all of my heart for four years," she wrote. "Without you, I cannot go on living. I must be your wife or surely I will die... perhaps by hanging myself."

The new letter was the latest in a series of flowery and increasingly desperate overtures to him, inviting him to tea. He knocked on the door of the house where she was renting a room and shortly thereafter sat across from Antonina in the parlour.

She poured tea for both of them. "Sugar?" she asked brightly.

"I prefer it black," he replied, "and bitter."

At this she smiled as if he had been making a joke. He sipped the tea slowly. "Do you know what my new opera is about, madam?"

She shook her head, grinning vacuously.

"It's from a novel by Aleksandr Pushkin called *Eugene Onegin*. It's about a man who rejects a woman who declares her undying love for him. He breaks her heart with his cruelty. When he is much older, he realizes he made a terrible mistake. He dies a lonely, broken man."

Antonina popped up from her chair. "That sounds very nice," she straightened her long skirt. "I made some cakes for you, would you like..."

"No," he interrupted. "I do not want cake."

He had decided on his course before coming here and he was determined not to falter. "Antonina Ivanovna, your letters moved me. If you are willing to allow me complete freedom to be who I am, I would like to propose that we marry."

The young woman gasped. "Marry, me? Of course! Yes, yes, yes!"

"You do understand, we will... that is, I will be... more like a brother to you, than a demanding husband in our marriage bed?"

"Oh yes! Whatever you want, my dearest," she cried. "I will get us those cakes now!"

As his train pulled into Nicholas Station in Petersburg, Pyotr was still shaking. The long journey from Moscow had failed to calm his state of overwhelming anxiety from seventy-nine wretched days of being married. And seventy-nine nights of making excuses for not consummating their union. He thought perhaps somehow it would help him turn the corner on his true nature.

He was mistaken. He had to escape. A letter to his brother Anatoly quickly resulted in a concocted excuse for Pyotr to leave Moscow just as summer was giving way to autumn.

Disembarking from the carriage, Pyotr saw his brother on the platform.

"Pyotr!" Anatoly called, waving to him.

If he could, he would jump into Tolya's arms. But Pyotr could barely walk. He shuffled towards his brother just as he reached him and collapsed into his waiting arms.

Sometime later, Pyotr heard noises. The rattling of dishes? A match being struck? A fire crackling and a cork being popped? His eyes were still heavy, but with some effort he managed to peel them back.

"Tolya?" he whispered. "Where am I?"

"Petya, you're safe now, brother," Anatoly replied softly. "In Petersburg at the Grand Hotel. Are you hungry? I ordered breakfast."

Pyotr sat up a little. "The Grand Hotel, where I came with..."

"Your wife on your honeymoon, yes. I'm sorry, it was the closest hotel I could find from the station," Anatoly replied. "You passed out. You've been sleeping for almost two days."

"Thank you, Tolya, for looking after me."

His brother poured a cup of tea at the linen covered table, and carried it over to Pyotr on a tray beside a plate of sweet rolls and sliced fruit. The nourishment lifted his spirit a little.

"I was wrong," he sighed. "I thought I could perhaps..."

Pyotr's words trailed off. His mind was knotted in guilt and regret.

"You could perhaps what? Deny who you are?"

He stared at Anatoly sitting on the edge of the bed. Pyotr could see the caring and understanding in his brother's eyes. "I think I am finally beginning to understand," Pyotr responded quietly. "There is nothing more fruitless than wanting to be something which I am not by nature."

CHAPTER 12

The arrival of Nadezhda von Meck in the life of Tchaikovsky was not only a blessing for the composer, but also for future audiences. Her aid enabled Tchaikovsky to dedicate his attention fully to composing, relieving him of the worry of financial stability, a worry that had plagued him for many years. She also bolstered his morale, although they never met in person, a conscious decision on their part. Their correspondence showed a large mutual respect, and Tchaikovsky often referred to her as his 'best friend'. They kept their relationship private, a friendship that was to endure a very long time.

Von Meck's mark on the world wasn't limited to her generosity with Tchaikovsky. An extremely well-educated woman with a mastery of various languages and knowledge of literature and philosophy, she also supported other talented musicians, using her inherited fortune to ease the life of these artists, purely for the sake of culture.

Tchaikovsky would dedicate several works to her, even though in order to preserve the private nature of their relationship, the dedications were never direct. The first of these was his Fourth Symphony, composed in 1877, one of few works that

Tchaikovsky maintained in high regard. Over the years to come after the composition of the symphony, his love for the work did not diminish as it did for many of his other works. Tchaikovsky would be his own worst critic during his lifetime, always demanding the absolute best of himself. In many cases, this would lead him to criticize his own work after it was finished, finding fault upon fault in the years passing by, a trait not uncommon in composers and, indeed, many artists.

Thanks to the correspondence between Tchaikovsky and Von Meck, we have a detailed description of the Fourth Symphony's structure and formation from the composer's personal perspective. Though he found it difficult to put in words on paper, Tchaikovsky described to her in detail the underlying emotions that drove the musical development of the symphony.

Central to the Fourth Symphony was the concept of 'Fate', which he described as 'the sword of Damocles', always hovering and never to be truly escaped. Musically, he employed a short but striking motif that is first stated in various brass sections as the theme for Fate. The observant listener will be reminded of the opening of Beethoven's Fifth Symphony, which uses a similar approach to the statement and repetition of its main theme. Tchaikovsky writes that he modelled his Fourth Symphony after 'the basic idea' of Beethoven's Fifth, a resemblance that is hard to miss in light of this information.

MEMORIES FROM DAYS GONE BY

Tchaikovsky describes the sentiment that fuels his symphony in more detail to Von Meck, pointing out melodies that serve to resurface one's memories of youth, and the return of the 'fate' theme to illustrate how mercilessly fate breaches back into the world of memories and longing for days gone by. He describes the final movement of the symphony as encouragement to find joy in the joy of others, which is accentuated through its fiery nature and the use of a Russian folk song as a secondary theme to its original first theme of Fate.

Further description of Tchaikovsky's Fourth Symphony would be inadequate in comparison to experiencing the work firsthand. Tchaikovsky's letter to Nadezhda von Meck, dating from February—March 1878, contains a detailed description of the symphony and its underlying emotions, making it a perfect companion to keep close while listening to this masterpiece.

As indicated previously, Tchaikovsky struggled with the more traditional Western musical forms. With his Fourth Symphony he breaks further with these traditional forms, convinced that the strength of the underlying emotions leads to a musical expressivity that cannot be contained in the stricter traditional forms. Though he does not fully abandon the overall structure of the Western form, he deviates often and strongly from its more detailed guidelines throughout the work. Examples include the statement of the second subject in a remote minor key instead of the 'prescribed' relative major of F minor (Ab major), and completely omitting the expected restatement of material in later sections throughout the symphony.

In the Fourth Symphony, one particular talent of Tchaikovsky became an additional factor diverting his work from traditional form: his unique gift for melody. In this work, he lets this talent rage in full fury, leading to gorgeous melodic flows that are so characteristic of his writing. However, contrary to established Western practices, his melodies are much more complete and fully fleshed out at their introduction. This prevents further development as was common in the established Western practices, where melodies would spring from smaller motifs and themes that grow throughout the work. This traditional approach can be compared to watching a time-lapse of a seed growing into a blooming flower, where we witness its growth as part of the piece.

Tchaikovsky, however, gives much less attention to this development throughout the Fourth Symphony, spinning complete melodies into existence out of the blue (compared to the much slower evolution common in Western symphonic form). As a result, Tchaikovsky had to rely on other techniques, such as variation, restatements, and modulations to substitute for true development, as the themes introduced simply had little room to evolve further from their initial statement. Though this certainly raised hairs and eyebrows among the musical traditionalists, had Tchaikovsky kept to these traditional prescriptions, his Fourth Symphony would likely not have been the masterpiece it was. His deliberate deviation from such practices, fuelled by the emotional turmoil underlying the work, allowed him to fully showcase not only his unparalleled gift for melody, but also his breathtaking emotional harmonies and textures.

The Fourth Symphony received a mix of praise and criticism. For some, the abandonment of traditional Western form led to a chaotic piece that felt incoherent and, at times, overly long. The title of "Fourth Symphony" certainly had something to do with this, as it suggested a work more in line with the established practices of the symphony form. These detours from convention led to various sharp criticisms that the symphony was confusing, crude, and even semi-barbaric. The lack of more elaborate melodic development in favour of fully stated melodies also led to harsh criticisms.

Nevertheless, the overall reception grew warmer and more enthusiastic, and to this day the Fourth Symphony is still considered one of the best symphonies by his hand, and rightfully so. As Tchaikovsky freed himself from the shackles of expected form and structure, his genius in melodic flow and emotionally rousing harmonies shines like a blazing sun from the piece, fully deserving the praise and recognition of audiences everywhere.

CHAPTER 13
CLARENS, SWITZERLAND, OCTOBER 1877
(AGE 37)

The crisp morning air of Lake Geneva filled Pyotr's lungs like a healing tonic. His early morning walks along the shore had gotten longer each day since Anatoly had brought him here last week. Pyotr stopped a moment, gazing over the dark lake. The sunlight sparkled innocently on the water, asking nothing of him save to share a moment of tranquility.

He breathed slowly and deeply. The warmth of the rising sun playing over his face seemed a transcendent gift from a benevolent Creator. If his days were to end now, poor as he was from a pecuniary perspective, he would die rich in the knowledge his music had saved at least one soul.

"You have been able to infuse a life into one so nearly at the end of her days as to be practically already dead," Nadezhda von Meck had written to him. "Your music, Pyotr Ilyich, throws me into a state of blissful madness; a condition in which one loses consciousness of all that is bitter and offensive in life. Listening to such music, I seem to soar above all earthly thoughts, my temples throb, my heart beats wildly, a mist swims before my eyes and my ears drink in the enchantment of the music. I feel that all is well with me, and I do not want to be reawakened. Ah,

God, how great is the man who has power to give others such moments of bliss!"

How could it be? A woman so interested in him she claimed to know where he was and what he was doing at any time on any day.

And yet, she wanted to know him only through the exchange of letters?

"The more you fascinate me, the more I shrink from knowing you," Nadezhda confessed. "It seems to me I could not then talk to you as I do now if we met unexpectedly. I prefer to think of you from a distance, to hear you speak and to be at one with you in your music."

Pyotr glanced back at the imposing edifice of the Villa Richelieu, softened by the morning haze. Something about the grandeur of the building dwarfed him as he reflected on the contrasts in his relationships with women. Though he had never met Nadezhda, he felt as if she occupied an empty place in his heart, even if they shunned physical contact.

Touching her would somehow spoil everything, lessen the bond between them and the joy they brought to each other. They were two strangers, closer than most married couples sleeping together every night.

His own wife Antonina by contrast was the real stranger. She knew neither his needs nor his aspirations. Had he used her simply as a way to cover the truth of his nature, hidden behind the shield of matrimony?

As he walked back to the hotel, he tried to find some beacon of hope. He only had enough money for a few more weeks. And then he would have to return to Moscow, resume his duties at the conservatory. Set aside composing and take care of a wife he would never love.

Or maybe, he could just disappear and fade from the memory of everyone who knew him. His only regret would be Nadezhda's tears.

"Pyotr!" a voice called out as he made his way toward the entrance of the hotel. "Come, quickly!"

It was his brother Anatoly, waving at him and there was someone standing beside him. Was it... no, wait... Nicholas Rubinstein?

Pyotr hurried towards both men, surprised at seeing his old friend here.

"Nicholas?" Pyotr exclaimed. "I don't know how you found me, but I'm so glad you did!"

Nicholas smiled. "As am I, maestro."

"He brought something for you," Anatoly exclaimed. "Come, let's go inside. Breakfast is waiting."

"Brought something?"

Nicholas reached inside his coat and pulled out an envelope. "A letter from Madam Nadezhda von Meck." He handed it to Pyotr. "I explained to her your... financial predicament."

Pyotr studied the thick envelope. His full name was inked in the elegant hand he had come to treasure these past months.

"She asked me to deliver it personally," Nicholas said, "and arranged my transport."

For a moment Pyotr wondered if he should review this in private, but these two men were like his guardian angels. He opened the envelope carefully and gasped when he unfolded the document inside to reveal a wad of banknotes.

He read the accompanying letter, heart galloping in his throat:

"My dearest friend,

Are we really such strangers?

Do you not realize how much I care for you? How I wish you all good? In my opinion, it is not the tie of sex or kindred which gives these rights, but the sense of mental and spiritual communion.

You know how many happy moments you have given me, how grateful I am, how indispensable you are to me, and how necessary it is that you should remain just as you were created? Consequently, what I do is not done for your sake, but for mine.

Why should you spoil my pleasure in taking care of you, and make me feel that I am not very much to you after all? You hurt me. If I wanted something from you, of course you would give it to me—is it not so?

Do not interfere with my management of your domestic economy, Pyotr Ilyich.

From this day forward, I kindly implore you to accept an annual allowance from me of 6,000 rubles. I apologize in advance for the pretence of such a gesture, but pray in the quiet solitude of my heart, you will understand.

Yours, with devotion and respect, N. F."

Pyotr clutched the letter and closed his eyes. Though he would prefer not to accept such an indenture, there was something more important than his pride.

The music inside of him yet to be born.

THE NEXT MORNING PYOTR AWOKE EARLY AND HURRIED FROM his room down to breakfast. He was bursting with an energy long departed. His fourth symphony rumbled inside him, restless, demanding, unyielding... as only a thing in F minor could do.

His opera *Eugene Onegin,* also unfinished, would have to wait. But that he would complete it was no longer in doubt. Nadezhda had lifted the slab of granite crushing him in the never-ending pursuit of rubles. He could crawl out now, pen in hand and devote himself to the only lover who never cheated on him, a mistress created from the purest form of passion, perfection so everlasting that time could not ravage it, nor death extinguish it.

Music.

Much still remained for him to do. All he had accomplished

so far was poor and imperfect, compared to what he could... no, what he *must* do in the future. Nadezhda had bestowed upon him the most precious of gifts.

The freedom to create. She was the angel of his heart, the patron of his soul, the one to whom he would dedicate all his future works...

"Petya!" his brother Anatoly called out.

Pyotr had wandered into the hotel's dining hall so absorbed he scarcely knew where he was. A musical phrase danced in his head, perhaps born of the possibilities afforded by his new station.

"Join us!" Nicholas implored, standing up at a table near the window that afforded a glorious panorama of the misty lake and the black mountains of Savoy rising to the heavens.

After tea was poured Pyotr remembered what he wanted to ask Nicholas. "Did you get my letter?" he asked. "My sketch pad, I had notes for my new symphony but stupidly, I left it at home."

"Home?" Nicholas repeated, glancing at Anatoly. The two men locked eyes, frowning at each other.

"Home in Moscow?" Nicholas asked. "With your... *wife?*"

Pyotr sighed. "Yes. I had all my notes, the first three movements of my new symphony in sketch form, and was set to work on a new orchestral effect, something I designed myself."

"I know your work is important," Anatoly said softly, "but your wife is still..." Now it was his turn to sigh.

"Still what?"

Nicholas leaned closer and touched Pyotr's arm. "We went to see her last week and explained that you are never going back to her."

"And how did she," Pyotr asked slowly, "...respond?"

Anatoly coughed. "Nicholas was quite direct. In fact, it made me go both hot and cold in the same moment. He told her you were going mad. That you needed acute psychological care and would rather drown yourself in the Volga than lay with her in the intimacies of your marriage bed."

Pyotr gasped. "Nicholas! Was that not rather too dramatic?"

"I'm afraid it was not," he replied, pouring himself more tea. "She said she belongs only to you. And while she knows she cannot compete with your music, she will wait for you in Moscow until you come home." He sipped his tea thoughtfully. "Whenever that might be."

Something inside Pyotr snapped. In that fleeting moment, a chorus of voices exploded inside him. The first bars of a scherzo called out, a conductor's baton tapped sharply.

"I'm not going back home," he said, rising from the table, glancing at the mountains behind Lake Geneva demanding to be conquered. "I neither wish, nor am I able, to return to Russia."

STANDING INSIDE THE LARGEST CHURCH IN THE WORLD, THE hallowed hall atop the burial site of the first Bishop of Rome, Pyotr was reduced to silence. The heavenly sunlight, streaming through three massive windows high atop the facade of the entrance, lit the vestibule with a light so divine it seemed to emanate from the eyes of God himself.

Despite the spectacle, and Pyotr's deep personal attachment to Christ, all the joy and wonders of Italy were wasted on this tour with Anatoly. They had left Switzerland a few weeks ago, with Pyotr's new circumstances affording him an opportunity to finally plot his own future.

"I feel quite sick," he whispered, as they shuffled along the granite floors of the church in a line of sweaty pilgrims. "I can't be around all these people another minute."

Outside of the basilica, even the gentle warmth of Rome's November sun was of little consolation. A splendid dinner and a walk among cascading fountains livened with colourful street vendors all proved useless in lifting his spirits.

"What's wrong, Petya?" his brother asked as they sat drinking wine and shelling roasted chestnuts. "I thought you loved this country?"

"I do. And I always will, but," Pyotr glanced across the piazza. "I'm not fit for a tourist's life. I see only the bad side of Rome. The beauties of the city are veiled to my eyes."

Anatoly nodded. "You have been depressed this whole trip. You were annoyed in Florence, and I suppose Venice will be no different?"

"Probably not. I imagined the sunshine, and the art and the gastronomy, the *dolce vita* here would propel my pen," he shook his head, biting down on his lip, "but I am at heart a northerner. I yearn for wide horizons and the unbounded expanse of the plains... at least in my mind."

His brother was often difficult to read, but today annoyingly transparent. "You're still running away, are you not? From your wife? I fear wherever you find yourself, another vista will seem preferable. Does she cast her shadow so wide upon you? Why does your distaste for her impel you against such a sword of despair?"

Anatoly was right of course, as he usually was about such matters. "She is not to blame for wanting to be a good wife and even a friend to me," Pyotr responded. "It's not her fault I did not find what I was looking for."

"Then let her go, *Petya*," Anatoly scolded. "Provide her with compensation and let me help arrange a divorce – not just on paper, but from the torment of your being."

CLARENS, SWITZERLAND, MARCH 1878 *(AGE 37)*

YOUNG KOLYA SIPPED HIS HOT CHOCOLATE SLOWLY AND smiled from across the table. "This is like drinking heaven," he intoned, lowering the cup slowly onto the wooden table. Much of the whipped cream that Pyotr had spooned on top of the hot drink now covered the boy's lip as a foamy moustache.

Pyotr laughed. "Delicious divinity," he scribbled on the pad of paper lying between them.

Koyla licked away some of his moustache. "Mmmm," he giggled. "Heaven tastes good!"

That the boy could talk was nothing short of a miracle. Just a few years ago Kolya was both deaf and mute. Now at nearly ten years old, he was an accomplished reader and talked clearly enough to be easily understood.

The time together the first week of March with Kolya and Modest back at the Villa Richelieu had cemented the boy's place in Pyotr's heart. His brother had done a miraculous job of developing Kolya's intellect, widening his perspective and laying out a bright future.

Still, Modest's lack of discretion was disconcerting. While Pyotr tried to keep his 'inclinations' hidden, Modest openly flaunted his desire for men. Tonight, he left Kolya with Pyotr to spend the night with a handsome new friend he met at the Villa spa shortly after they arrived.

Pyotr scolded him on the way out. "A man who falls into the embrace of any passing trash cannot be the educator you strive to become," he warned Modest who hung his head, but refused to change his evening plans.

Pyotr glanced at Kolya, watching the two brothers from his silent world of deafness. Even so, Pyotr thought it better to whisper. "I do not want evil tongues to wound an innocent child. Sodomy and pedagogy cannot abide in harmony with one another."

Much later that night, after Kolya was tucked in bed and fast asleep, Pyotr tried to focus only on his work.

His Fourth Symphony, which he secretly dedicated to Nadezhda, was finished. "This work is an unburdening of the soul in music, in the same manner in which a poet expresses himself in verse," he wrote to her. "It is about fate, the force which prevents happiness from attaining its goal. Jealousy ensures happiness shall not be complete. Fate is an invincible force that can never be overcome — merely endured."

Likewise, his opera *Eugene Onegin* that he couldn't help but associate with his estranged wife Antonina, was now complete. He had let the story of a man who spurns the love of an intelligent woman seduce him into proposing to Antonina. But she was no Tatyana, and unlike the fictional Eugene Onegin broken by rejecting such a woman of profound depth, Pyotr was haunted by his fleeting decision to correct the wrongs of a fictional character.

Regardless, the opera was done. Last week he had sent it off to Nicholas Rubinstein in Moscow. Tonight, he would work a little more on his Grand Sonata, which for some reason was not coming easily. He found himself struggling to force weak and feeble ideas from his mind, agonizing over each and every bar.

But perhaps, if he kept at it, inspiration would eventually strike.

After he poured himself a strongly brewed cup of tea, he got set to begin when there was a sharp knock on the door of his room. The hotel's night maid was always checking in on him about this time and he cursed the interruption. But when he opened the door, it was not the maid, but the familiar face of the one who still haunted his dreams.

"I have come a long way," Iosif Kotek said quietly standing in the door holding his violin case. "I know I am not worthy, but I hold on to the foolish fantasy that there is still a place for me in your life."

Iosif was like a creature possessed, coaxing music from his violin. Pyotr played along with him on the piano in the empty theatre of the Villa Richelieu while a fierce winter storm kept guests at bay.

This was the third day since Iosif's arrival in Clarens and though they'd shared only a tender hug and light kiss, performing music together was as intimate as anything they had ever done. They shed tears of joy playing the *Symphonie Espagnole,* a new work by Éduoard Lalo. Iosif had just received the score from Paris.

Whatever quarrels Pyotr and Iosif had previously, whatever jealousies lingered, all was forgiven and forgotten in the exchange of musical harmonies. Like the scar on Iosif's damaged finger, their emotional rift was but a faint memory. After nearly thirty minutes of playing without a break they paused, flushed, their hair clinging to the dew on their foreheads.

"This music is so light, so fresh. The piquant rhythms, the perfectly written melodies, it's almost like," Pyotr exclaimed, searching for a suitable equivalent, "like a French soufflé – risen to perfection in a Spanish oven."

Iosif smiled. "Beats sausage and sauerkraut any day."

"Jawohl!" Pyotr replied. "The Germans are fading. God bless Bach and Beethoven, but now they're getting too heavy. Too old... too, too much. They're at a dead end, but the French..."

Suddenly a thought seized him. "I need my pen! My sketch pad!"

Iosif leaned closer. "Why?"

"I have an idea. A violin concerto! Perhaps in..."

"D major?" Iosif lifted his violin and stroked his bow.

"Yes!" Pyotr ran to find his pen and pad. "It begins as an allegro, floating weightless above the clouds."

As Pyotr continued spouting ideas, Iosif improvised on the violin. Then Pyotr sat at the piano overflowing with the spirit of creation and allowed the music to soar out of him.

FOR THE NEXT THREE WEEKS PYOTR POURED ALL THAT WAS most precious to him into the violin concerto. Five days of playing with Iosif and the first movement was complete. Three days later the second, and finally, eleven nights after they began, all that remained was for the work to be played from beginning to end, then copied to paper.

"Everything I am lives hidden inside this work," Pyotr said quietly from his seat at the piano. He watched Iosif adjusting the strings of his violin as they prepared to play through the concerto tonight in the empty dining hall of the Villa Richelieu Hotel.

It was almost midnight. Outside the picture window, a full moon set the lake ablaze in translucent glory.

Together they began in D major, playing through the lyrical *Allegro*, moving onto the *Canzonetta* in the distant and unexpected voice of G minor. They finished back in D major for the lively *Finale*, its melodies building upon descending fourths, echoing the harmonies of so many Russian folksongs pulsing inside Pyotr.

Thirty-five minutes later the last bar of the violin concerto resonated through the empty dining hall. Moonlight lapped softly on the lake. Pyotr hung his head, overcome with the wonder of the composition that had somehow sprung from his pen seemingly fully-formed.

Iosif laid his violin down on top of the piano. He leaned over and touched Pyotr's chin. Their wet eyes locked as they moved their faces closer together until their tears intertwined.

Although Pyotr had been careful up until now to avoid temptation, stung by the hotel staff's rude gossip, his self-imposed vows were fading quickly.

"Petya," Iosif whispered as he touched his lips against Pyotr's, "our musical communion is complete."

Inside Pyotr's room, they consummated their old passion deep into the night until they drifted into the embrace of sleep just as dawn rose contentedly in the eastern sky.

It was well past noon when Pyotr was awoken by knocking

on the door. It was likely the maid, come to make up the room. She had a key and unless he opened the door quickly...

"*Herr Tschaikowsky?*" the maid called in her stern German voice. He tried to yank the covers over his bare chest. She jumped when she saw him. "*Entschuldigung!*"

The maid stared at Iosif laying naked on his back, oblivious to her lingering examination. "Sorry," she whispered in halting Russian. "I come back... later."

She took another long look at Iosif, snoring softly in all his naked glory. A frown washed over her face before she raised her eyebrows at Pyotr, shook her head disapprovingly, then retreated from the room, slamming the door loudly behind her like a wooden exclamation mark.

Pyotr lay back on his pillow. He released a deep sigh.

When Iosif finally awoke almost an hour later, Pyotr's elation from the night before was gone. There was a bitter taste to the day.

"Why the long face?" Iosif asked as he sat up on the bed. Pyotr was already dressed, standing at the credenza, starting to copy the violin concerto for orchestration.

"The world is hateful," Pyotr replied without looking up.

Iosif, still naked, padded over to him. "Our concerto?" he asked as he wrapped his arms around Pyotr and peered over his shoulder at the cover page.

Iosif froze.

"Leopold Auer?" Iosif read the name like a prescription for poison, releasing Pyotr from his arms. "You're dedicating our..." Iosif paused a moment, his anger enveloping the room, "our concerto... to him?"

Pyotr hung his head. He said nothing but felt his cheeks warming. "I had no choice. It should be you, of course, but the price we would pay..."

"*You* would pay!" Iosif snapped. He sat back down on the bed, hands on his knees glaring. "We birthed this child together. Now you cast its father to hell!"

"No, *kotik*..."

"I am not your *kotik*!" Iosif shouted. "You've found a new plaything. Go see if Leopold will share your bed." He grabbed his shirt and pants, and headed for the door, his naked backside taunting Pyotr with a rude smirk. "He certainly won't be able to play your... your horrible concerto!"

With that he stepped out, slammed the door and shouted. "No one will!"

SIMAKI, RUSSIA - AUGUST 1879 (AGE 39)

"BY NATURE I AM A SAVAGE."

Pyotr repeated the proclamation to himself as he stepped out of the cottage for his daily walk through the forest surrounding the estate of Nadezhda von Meck. The guest house was a fair distance from the main estate where he had stayed a number of times at her insistence.

But only when she was away.

However, this time she was at home with her children and offered Pyotr the use of her plush guest house in the woods for as long as he cared to stay. The few miles separating them at present were as close to each other as they had ever been.

"My whole life long I have been a martyr to my enforced relations with society," he wrote to her recently. "By nature I am a savage. Every new acquaintance, every fresh contact with strangers, has been the source of acute moral suffering."

He recalled her reply, praying she did not add to his torments, repeating her vow that they should never meet. Their relationship transcended the fleeting, and ultimately disappointing, physical in favour of the everlasting and perfect spiritual.

Pyotr wandered slowly through the deserted path, spotting the dark faces of black mushrooms and grey fungi that fed off the forest's rot and decay. He stopped a moment touching his churning stomach, so full of acid and gas. His bad digestion and the constant bouts of the catarrh that clogged his throat and nose gave him pause to agree with Nadezhda.

He longed for Nirvana. He was getting too stout. His nerves were falling to pieces. He was doubtful he could be anything more than a selfish bachelor, living a dull, narrow, lifeless existence. Even his compositions seemed to be stagnating in their pale indifference.

He stooped down and picked one of the large mushrooms clothed in powdery black felt.

"Were I to vanish from the face of the earth to-day," he explained to the wilting fungi, "it would be no great loss to Russian music and would certainly cause no one great unhappiness."

Antonina would not agree to a divorce, leaving him anxious and depressed.

Leopold Auer refused to perform his violin concerto rejecting the dedication of the piece, proclaiming it "unplayable."

Likewise, Iosif refused to ever perform the concerto again. Pyotr's new opera, 'The Maid of Orleans' was done and although he had squeezed music out of his brain for months on end, the finished work did not agree with him.

And likely no one else either.

"In a word, there are many thorns, and few roses," he told the uncaring mushroom. Could something that fed off decay, and preferred darkness to sunlight, ever die? Or would it just shrivel up like him, until no trace of its existence was left behind?

He crushed the thing in his hands and began to walk along the larger path that eventually led to the von Meck estate.

He was startled when he heard the sound of horses approaching. A parade of three open carriages clattered noisily as they hastened down the cobblestone path. A refined looking woman sat in the back seat of the lead carriage as it pulled closer and then stopped in front of him before he could move out of the way.

Nadezhda?

He froze staring at the woman who was not only his benefactor, but his dear, dear friend. He had seen her portrait many times.

They stared at each other as the driver of the carriage greeted him. Pyotr tipped his hat, bowed slightly and tried to avert his eyes. Nadezhda smiled awkwardly, nodded to Pyotr and placed her hand over her heart. He did the same, and then stepped aside.

Without a word, she motioned for the driver to proceed down the road leaving Pyotr behind, still holding what remained of the crushed and broken black mushroom in his hand.

NICE, FRANCE - MARCH 1881 (AGE 40)

PYOTR LAID THE TELEGRAM HE HAD JUST RECEIVED ON THE BED of his hotel room as he packed for Paris.

He recalled the last time he had seen Nikolay Rubinstein, a few months ago in Petersburg. They joked over oysters about the quality of the work Pyotr had just completed for the upcoming Moscow Exhibition.

"I'm undecided whether my overture for *The Year 1812* is good or bad," Pyotr mused. He reached for the last oyster on the tray, but instead offered it to his old friend who adored the freshly shucked delicacy. "But it is probably the latter."

Nikolay slurped the oyster with a sigh of contentment and washed it down with the rest of his wine. "Nonsense!" he smirked. "No work that climaxes with the blasting of a cannon can be judged bad by any critic – military or musical!"

They both laughed. "Perhaps," Pyotr replied, "but I wrote it without any warmth of enthusiasm. You know how much I loathe the glorification of..."

He was interrupted by Nikolay's hoarse coughing. He gripped his throat, his face turning a bright crimson. "Sorry," he gasped between choking fits, until he wrestled the disturbance under control.

Pyotr poured some water for him. "I thought you were on the mend?"

Nikolay shook his head. "No, not really. But don't worry. It's nothing."

Nothing? Pyotr thought, recalling how after that evening, they agreed to meet in Nice so that Nikolay could rest in a warmer climate. He re-read the urgent telegram from Paris:

Nikolay's situation has deteriorated.
We are afraid for his life.

How could it be? Nikolay, so full of life, so dedicated to Pyotr and his music, premiering and promoting every new work as if it were a true masterpiece? Nikolay, his protector, his champion; only a few years older, but so like a father.

Father?

Pyotr closed up his bag and hurried out of his room. Last year when he lost his father, Pyotr was saddened but heartened to know he passed peacefully after a full life of eight-five years. His angelic soul had surely risen to Heaven.

Was not Nikolay much too young to join him? Pyotr stopped at the front desk. He had telegraphed the Grand Hotel in Paris where Nikolay was staying, seeking an update.

"Are there any messages for me? I'm expecting a telegram," he asked the concierge. The man at the desk looked down, searching beneath the counter. The courier train was leaving for Paris within the hour, and with any luck Pyotr would soon be able to lend some comfort to Nikolay.

"Yes, sir," the concierge said. "This just arrived for you." He handed Pyotr a folded note, which consisted of only three words:

Rubinstein est mort.

The words burned his eyes as words filled his head. "Rubinstein is dead."

He could barely breathe as he walked away and without being aware of how he did so, made his way to the station and found a seat on the carriage. As the train pulled away, his head went dark.

Tsar Alexander II was dead, assassinated just a few weeks ago in Petersburg. Pyotr's dear Mama and Papa were gone. And now, Nikolay.

Life was fleeting. It was short. It was cruel. God could call you at any moment.

He stared out the window at the passing French countryside. His dear friend was gone, and there was much he should have told him when he had the chance. But there was another friend, perhaps even dearer, who could still hear his words.

He pulled out his sketch pad and drafted a note to Nadezhda. He recalled all his critics that Nikolay had railed against for so many years. And all those who had cast aspersions on his 'inclinations.'

Inclinations Nikolay had chosen to ignore.

Pyotr was filled with the need to bare his feelings to Nadezhda.

"It is as if we were specially created to fight against evil forever, to seek ideals, to strive for eternal truth - but never to reach the goal," he wrote. "At least, let us be lenient toward those who, in their blindness, love evil by inborn instinct. Do we have the right to repay them with evil for evil? No! we can only repeat with Christ, 'Lord, forgive them, for they know not what they do'."

He released all his despair to her, the one person left on this earth who accepted him without reservation and who preached his name would live long after he was gone.

> "An artist should not be troubled by the indifference of his contemporaries. If fame is destined for me, it will come with slow but sure steps."

He pulled the telegram from his pocket, stared at it a moment and closed his eyes.

Rubinstein est mort.

But not forgotten. Pyotr would find a way to honour him with a gift that would never die.

CHAPTER 14

As we have seen repeatedly, Tchaikovsky's creative choices were often received poorly by traditionalists. We only need to consider the criticism he had received from his mentors earlier in his musical career, accusing him of being "neither German nor Russian". Critics attending performances of his works throughout his musical career often seized upon the opportunity to deliver scathing remarks when they found the music lacking in what they considered 'the norm'.

Though it would be nice to think that Tchaikovsky shrugged off such scorning reviews with more and more ease as his career progressed, he would remain sensitive to these attacks throughout it. The image of the sensitive artist certainly applied to our tortured hero.

Nevertheless, he did become more confident in his creative decisions as the years passed. He realized that adherence to traditional practices hindered the musical storm within him, and he understood that even though some form of common structure was helpful at a higher level of abstraction, strict adherence to more detailed rules and guidelines simply was not conducive to his creative genius (even if he would probably never use those words himself).

His Violin Concerto in D major is another wonderful example of this battle between form and creativity. Once again, Tchaikovsky starts by introducing a theme that is not heard again after its introduction, similar to his approach to his first piano concerto. After this, the violin bursts forth into a highly melodious torrent that lasts throughout the first movement with no holds barred. His decoration and variation of the extremely expressive melodies that seem to gush from the instrument lead to a breathtakingly gorgeous soloist performance.

One might suspect that this musical maelstrom resembles his inner turmoil in this period of his life, a suspicion strengthened by the enthusiasm and energy with which he approached the compositional process. The first movement of the concerto was written in a mere matter of days. The instrumentation of the concerto is well suited to highlight the prominent soloist performance, featuring mostly woodwinds, strings, a light brass setting (only two trumpets and four horns), and minimal percussion in the form of two timpani. All this allows the solo violinist to take centre stage without being overshadowed in any way by the orchestra. Especially in the first movement, the orchestra functions mainly for accentuation and colour, letting the solo part dance and rage above it.

In the second movement of the concerto (the canzonetta), soloist and orchestra come closer together. Though the violin keeps centre stage, it's more subdued compared to the fiery melodic dance in the first movement, creating contrast between the movements. The interplay between solo violin and orchestra is more prominent, and the sense of call-and-response between them is heightened. Where the orchestra serves more of a background function in the first movement, letting the violin dazzle and flash its way through fast melodic passages and progressions of double stops, in the canzonetta there seems to be more balance between soloist and orchestra.

Even though this description might suggest a tamer section, the expressive melodic lines in this movement captivate the

listener's attention from start to finish, and the movement is in
no sense less enchanting than the first. In fact, the sense of
melancholy that permeates the second movement might have an
even bigger appeal to some than the virtuosic solo performance
of the violin in the first.

DANCE WILL NOT BE DENIED

Our sense of repose and calm is, however, then immediately
shattered as both orchestra and violin burst into the third and
final movement without pause. Here, the composer sweeps the
audience off its feet with vigorous dancelike themes and
rhythms. The attentive observer will see members of the
orchestra nodding along with a smile in many performances to
be found online; the dance will simply not be denied. Listeners
may very well close their eyes and find themselves caught up in
the crowd of a lively Russian feast, the masses dancing in exhila-
ration. Though the third movement may seem deceptively
simple compared to the first two, it is nevertheless a display of
virtuosity, both in performance and composition.

Tchaikovsky originally dedicated the Violin Concerto in D to
the renowned violin teacher, player, conductor, and composer
Leopold Auer. It is sometimes said that Auer thought the
concerto to be unplayable. This rumour is not entirely accurate.
As a violinist, Auer found parts of the work somewhat less suited
to the nature of the violin as an instrument. He would later
rework these passages to better match the intentions of the
composer with the characteristics of the violin, thus making the
effects intended by Tchaikovsky more prominent than in the
original version.

This process of refinement also occurs in piano concerti,
where a professional pianist might also be inclined to make alter-
ations to make better use of the possibilities and characteristics
of the instrument. After all, Tchaikovsky was not a concert

pianist or violinist, so it's only natural he might not have considered the more practical aspects of performance like a professional player might do. The edited version by Auer can still be found today for those interested.

That the violin concerto is a fiendishly difficult piece remains a fact (some even consider Auer's version to be more difficult at times than Tchaikovsky's). Then again, if difficult pieces were never performed, the musical world would have missed out on Paganini's Caprices, Sibelius's concerto, and Beethoven's "Kreutzer" Sonata, to name only a few of the world's most fiendishly difficult masterworks.

Like much of Tchaikovsky's work, critical opinions differed, and not all thought the concerto a masterpiece, difficult or not. Famous and influential critic Eduard Hanslick proclaimed it a piece 'whose stink one can hear', and 'odorously Russian'. With regards to the violin performance, he found the instrument 'not played, but beaten black and blue'. It may not come as a surprise that Hanslick belonged to the camp of traditionalists, and that as such he found the second movement much more to his liking. Unfortunately for Hanslick and his fellow conservatives, the sweeping finale of the concerto crushed whatever hopes they may have had for a more traditional approach.

The snobbish criticism (for it's hard to call it otherwise) does make one wonder what exactly music critics hope to achieve; a judgement based on the musical and creative merits of a piece is certainly not always the goal. Reviews like those by Hanslick and others throughout Tchaikovsky's career certainly show that, at least to the critics, it is more important that a piece is proper and high class (read: traditional) than that the music is to be enjoyed, whether it be simple or complex, folksy or sophisticated. Let us simply be thankful that Tchaikovsky chose to follow his own creativity over convention and tradition.

THE YEAR 1812 SOLEMN OVERTURE

Creativity, however, can be hard to force into being. Whereas Tchaikovsky was able to pour his musical thoughts into the violin concerto, 'The Year 1812 Solemn Overture' (more popularly known as the '1812 Overture') was quite another matter. The work in E-flat major did not spring forth from his genius as the violin concerto had done. He confided to Nadezhda von Meck and various others that he considered a work commissioned to celebrate the opening of an exhibition a completely uninspiring undertaking. Though it's hard to deny that the work itself certainly has a rousing patriotic feel to it, a sense of glory and victory, it is in many ways quite unlike other works by the maestro. It is considerably more noisy and more linear than many of his other works, and the composer himself proclaimed that he had extraordinarily little love for the piece. Perhaps he would not have undertaken the task at all if the request had not been a personal one from Nikolay Rubinstein.

The overture has a simple structure and leaves little to the imagination. The background story revolved around Napoleon's invasion of Russia. After a victory against the Russian troops at Borodino, Napoleon and his army marched on to Moscow. The battle had been won at great costs, and Napoleon's resources were extremely low. Upon arriving in Moscow, he found the city partially burned and quite abandoned. Any hope of replenishing supplies and making it through the winter was dashed on the spot, and the French were ultimately forced to retreat. Disease, extreme weather, and skirmishes all along the lines further thinned out the French army. All in all, hardly the outcome Napoleon had hoped for. It was an extremely nasty turn for the French in a war that at Borodino had seemed to sway in their favour.

The overture mirrors these events. Solemn strings play a melody known from an Eastern Orthodox hymn, symbolising the Russians' desire for a swift salvation from the French invasion. Throughout this section, melodies from La Marseillaise come into the forefront. Though La Marseillaise is certainly the French national anthem these days, and had been until 1805, Napoleon had banned its use during his reign, and it's highly unlikely that it was played at the time of the invasion. However, it was once again made the French national anthem in 1879, a few years before the request from Rubinstein to Tchaikovsky.

The Russian musical elements and La Marseillaise compete for attention for a while in the work, before the French melodies begin to grow more glorious and triumphant, overshadowing their Russian counterparts. The score calls for the sound of cannon shots, a reference to the battle at Borodino, after which the piece turns into a long downwards run. The reference to the French retreat is hard to be ignored here, especially as we once again hear the hymn which had originally started the piece. A grand finale, employing even more cannon shots, loud and jubilant percussion (including church bells), and the melody of the then national anthem of Russia: 'God save the Tsar!'

As mentioned earlier, the piece leaves little to the imagination, and is an unusual work by Tchaikovsky's hand from an artistic point of view. However, for its intended use it was an excellent fit, displaying exactly the bombastic grandeur that one might expect at the opening of an exhibition dedicated to the Russian victory over the French invaders.

The use of artillery in a musical piece is certainly not common (though one can imagine how it became a part of the work, considering the backstory), and in a practical sense made live performances faithful to the original score quite difficult. Artillery was never specifically designed to be a precisely timed instrument, so over the many years since its conception, many interesting alternatives have been used, ranging from recordings of cannon shots to bass drums and sledgehammers. Interestingly, Mahler would later incorporate a similar technique in his Sixth Symphony, which has led to the birth of the Mahler hammer, an instrument which can still be found in certain orchestral settings.

Though the 1812 Overture is certainly one of Tchaikovsky's most well-known works, it cannot be said to be his most artistic work. It certainly does not conjure the magical and enchanting atmosphere of works such as Swan Lake, nor does it show the composer's amazing gift for melodic lines as in his Fourth Symphony. The complete collection of Tchaikovsky's compositions by Tchaikovsky's hand is enormous, and any lover of music is bound to encounter various pieces that will in some way take hold over them. For those wishing to understand more, the composer himself has provided useful insight into his views on harmony and music with the 'Guide to the Practical Study of Harmony', written during his time as a professor at the Moscow Conservatory.

Despite (or perhaps, thanks to) his struggles of form versus creativity, Tchaikovsky's constant switching between Russian and German musical identities, and continued criticism from traditionalists and conservatives, it is undeniable that Tchaikovsky was a composer of extreme musical genius.

CHAPTER 15

PETERSBURG, RUSSIA - OCTOBER 20, 1893
(AGE 53)

Even in sleep, Pyotr sensed the fragility of each beat of his dying heart. He drifted in and out of consciousness, fitful against the cold, impersonal sheets and hard mattress of the small bed. The face of an old friend fluttered before him, then turned away.

"Nadezhda Filaretovna! Why do you forsake me?"

A stabbing pain woke him. Her face evaporated.

"Pyotr?" a breath whispered, "the doctors want to..."

"No!" he cried. "Nothing can they do!" He stared up at the ghostly outline of his brother.

"Your kidneys are failing," Modest sobbed. "A hot bath is ..."

"No, *Modi.*" Pyotr closed his eyes. "I shall not recover."

Modest wailed. A younger voice joined the chorus and for a second Pyotr was back in the concert hall, directing the orchestra. "Modi, would you grant me one final request?"

The weeping slowed. "Certainly." He felt his brother's hand upon his face. "What is it?"

"I need a piano, a cello, and a violin," Pyotr gasped as a pain gripped him. "Can... you..." he struggled to finish, "arrange it?"

There was no response. And then whispers. Finally, Modest

replied. "Of course, *Petya*... They are here now, awaiting your instruction."

"Thank... you," Pyotr mouthed, barely able to form the words. "Gentlemen, let's start with the piano trio."

Slowly the music rose and soon Pyotr was once again on stage of the Moscow Conservatory.

———

HEARTBROKEN STRINGS OF THE GRAND PIANO VIBRATED AS though they were presiding over a funeral. In some ways Pyotr felt it was just that, a requiem for dearly departed Nikolay Grigoryevich Rubinstein.

The rehearsal of his haunting Piano Trio, written and dedicated to his old friend, the great artist who'd died just over a year ago, was taking place on the same stage and on the same piano Nikolay himself used to premiere so many of Pyotr's works.

"He's here with us," Sergy Taneyev, the pianist playing through the opening movement spoke softly as he lifted his hands from the keys. Jan on violin and Wilhelm on cello dropped their bows.

The empty hall went quiet.

Pyotr nodded. "I feel him too." He searched the eyes of the pianist. "You think he would approve? I wrote it for him."

"He would indeed," Sergy replied, turning the first page of the sheet music arranged before him. "And I'm sure he would remind all the artists who play this composition, to conform *exactly* to the metronomic indications of the composer."

The pianist shot a menacing look at Jan and Wilhem who looked back at him bewildered.

"Sergy. Jan. Wilhelm," Pyotr replied. "Your enthusiasm gives me great pleasure." The violinist and cellist bowed their heads. "What Sergy says is true, but I would be deeply indebted if you applied your own enlightened gifts to this composition, as Nikolay used to advise his players."

Pyotr pointed to the ceiling high above them. "Please continue... for him."

The musicians began again, starting with the dark and brooding *Pezzo elegiaco* in A minor. Pyotr conducted the opening movement with Wilhelm's inspired performance of the opening cello solo. The strings mourned in sorrow and then forty minutes later, returned for the final, plaintive funeral-like march.

The bittersweet refrain echoed through the concert hall in memory of a man who found the beauty in each of Pyotr's compositions. Beauty that lay waiting to be discovered on every page.

His head swayed back and forth as the players ran through the last variation of his piano trio, shifting from A major to A minor until...

"It was the unboiled water," someone whispered as a pungent odour woke Pyotr. "We warned him, but he ignored us!"

Strong hands massaged his back and his chest. He was sitting in a strange little bed. Where had Modi taken the musicians?

Pyotr opened his eyes. Angels gathered round him.

"Maestro," one dressed like a nurse spoke. "The cholera has left you weak. The doctor is going to inject you, to help against the poisons building up inside you."

A jabbing pain made him flinch.

"It's musk and camphor," the angel nurse murmured. Her face glowed and he knew she was not of this world, but sent by his mother to guide him to the next.

"Thank you," he replied closing his eyes. "But you should rest. It's late, please don't fuss over me."

He needed the musicians again. "Modi," he whispered, as numbness swept over him. "Get them to play again. Please, brother?"

There was a moment of silence and then a familiar voice filled his ear. "They're here again, *Petya*... ready for you."

———

Sounds drifted in slowly — beneath, above and around the doors to the little chamber in Gatchina Palace where Pyotr waited nervously for his audience with the Emperor. Yes, it was indeed a great honour, as he had been reminded by many friends.

But why then was he so agitated? He held a bubbling glass of salts, praying another dose of bromide would regain himself enough to meet Alexander the Third in the flesh.

Too soon, the door opened, and he was loudly announced. "Pyotr Ilyich Tchaikovsky," a tenor voice rang out as Pyotr stood sheepishly, staring out at the colourfully dressed musicians and two tall, regal figures far off at the end of the cavernous hall.

He downed the bromide, set the glass aside, and strode towards the imposing bear of a man he recognized from portraitures as Tzar Alexander. The music began, swelling strains of his '1812 Overture' boldly announcing him better than his name could ever do.

Pyotr tensed as he made his way toward the Emperor and the Empress, stopping as he had been instructed, to bow his head before them.

The music played a few bars of the march he'd composed for Alexander's coronation last year, then ended dramatically while he kept his head bowed in respect.

"Pyotr Ilyich," the Emperor spoke in a voice both commanding and reassuring, "you are a true son of Russia."

As Pyotr straightened, he was taken slightly aback. The countenance of this man was not what Pyotr had envisioned. Though Alexander was a little taller than Pyotr who himself stood over six feet, he was much heavier — a truly dominating man. Still, the Emperor's dark eyes had a soft, sympathetic quality. A large cyst to the left of Alexander's nose made him seem an ordinary man, with blemishes no different than a working peasant in the countryside.

"Your music is all Maria Feodorovna talks about!" The Emperor smiled. "My wife and I both delight in…"

"More than delight," the woman standing beside Alexander interrupted.

Pyotr grinned. Only an Empress would cut short the words of a Tsar. "I am transformed by it, lifted from the bonds of mere existence to the heights of musical exultation."

He stood staring. Maria, the Empress and wife of Alexander, was even more of wonder than her husband. "Thank you, your Excellency. I am humbled and…" he struggled to find the right words, "quite speechless."

Alexander stepped closer and whispered. "Maria has been waiting all week for you, and I must admit, I too have been counting the days."

A guard stepped closer and handed Alexander a medal, draped over a velvet-covered plaque. The formal program was about to begin, announced with a short fanfare from the musicians.

"Pyotr Ilyich Tchaikovsky," the Emperor began, his voice resonating through the lavish drawing room, "in honour of your exemplary service to Russia, you are as of this day, Twenty-three, February, Eighteen Eighty-four, a member of the order of Saint Vladimir, Fourth Class," he boomed. "I, Alexander Alexandrovich Romanov, the Emperor of Russia, the King of Poland and the Grand Duke of Finland, do so bequeath this honour upon you."

The framed medal was a fine honour, but it was in the looks of the Emperor and the Empress that Pyotr found his true reward. With but a single moment of locking eyes with him, and one bewitching glance from her, Pyotr knew he would always remain their most loyal adherent.

They insisted he sit with them for a recital of his music as they continued to whisper their admiration in squeals of delight.

This was indeed the most royal day of his life. He laughed at their jokes and promised he had much, much more music left inside him.

As they talked, the orchestra began to play themes from *Swan Lake,* apparently at the request of the Empress. Maria leaned closer and made him vow to write another ballet. He promised her no less than the finest work of his life.

She touched his cheek with her angelic hand, "Pyotr Ilyich, I know it will be. We believe in you."

THE BLACK SWAN SPREAD HER WINGS UNTIL THE WORLD WENT dark. Muffled voices pierced her feathers.

"The only hope left is a hot bath," a stern voice whispered. "But, it is a very, very faint hope indeed."

Pyotr felt himself being lifted from the bed and slowly lowered into steaming, near scalding liquid. He was too weak to protest and prayed the sight of his withered form did not cause great discomfort to those attending him. Through the mist he thought he could see the face of his brothers and sisters – Niko-lai, Alexandra, Zinaida, Ippolit, Anatoly and Modest.

"Sasha?" he called out. "Are you still here? With me?"

A soft hand touched his shoulder. "She is with the angels, *Petya.*"

He remembered now. His little darling sister, Aleksandra, taken not long ago, buried at the monastery. "Modi, was I a poor brother to her?"

"No," Modest replied gently. "You were always in her heart. And I know she will forever live in yours."

Pyotr could feel his life force slipping away. His withered bowels were useless, his body absent of any sensation save for the tears, burning his eyes and searing the chapped skin of his face as they ran down his cheeks.

"I never learned to love," he whimpered. "I did not give or

receive." He began to sob. "My heart is broken." Regret sluiced from his lips, "I am broken."

His words lingered through the steam. "No, *Petya*," Modest finally responded. "You are more loved than you will ever know."

A violin began to play, accompanied by a piano.

Iosif?

How could it be? He was long gone from this world. "Is he here, playing for me?" Pyotr asked, trying to find a face through the steam.

"Playing for you?" Modest replied, hesitating. "I... I... oh, yes, yes. Of course, *Petya*. Of course he is."

DESPITE HIS CURRENT CONDITION, IOSIF'S VIOLIN REMAINED an extension of his limbs. Pyotr watched his dying friend perform, sitting on the edge of his small bed at the Spa Hotel in Davos, high up in the Swiss Alps.

Iosif insisted on playing. "Our concerto is not only playable, it is a gift I treasure," he pronounced after he finished. "My jealous heart undid me last time. For that I beg forgive..."

Pyotr was about to protest there was nothing to forgive, when Iosif began to cough violently.

Again.

For the past three days since arriving at the spa for deathly ill consumptive patients, Pyotr could only squeeze Iosif's hand as his friend hacked and wheezed until bloody spittle foamed about his mouth. His white shirt was stained with crimson splotches.

When Iosif finally regained control and tried to speak, Pyotr touched his lips to quiet him. "Shhhhh," Pyotr said, reaching for a towel to clean the bloody mess from Iosif's face. "I am here now."

He looked out the window at the snow-capped peaks. He'd been reading Lord Byron's *Manfred* on the long train ride from Moscow, and now the mountain taunted him like a stone-faced demon. The Alps seemed to embody the stoic torment of Manfred – the guilt of his dead, beloved Astarte.

Pyotr turned away from the uncaring cliff. "Iosif, you are not going to die. I'm not yet ready to let you go." Pyotr finished cleaning Iosif's face and laid the soiled cloth aside. "Let's get you dressed. I'm taking you to dinner and we'll go see a show."

A weak smile struggled to draw itself over Iosif's pale face. "Thank you, *Petya*. I do not deserve a friend like you."

Before Pyotr could respond, another coughing fit seized Iosif. This time a nurse and doctor were required to help him. But when it was finally over, Pyotr still insisted they dress Iosif and give him something to control his hacking seizures.

Not long after, they lingered over soup and *rosti*, slowly melting cheese from a glowing raclette, enjoying a fondue of beef and scallops – and finishing with coffee, fruit and chocolate. Later, they sat close together through a theatre show, laughing and smiling at each other, holding hands in the darkness.

The next day Pyotr bid Iosif adieu, promising to meet again soon in France or Italy or maybe even in Russia. They would ring in 1885 together, in grand style, wherever they might find themselves.

But two months later, after another painful night alone in his little bed in Davos, Iosif was dead.

And when Pyotr in Moscow received the news a few days later, he wished he was too. He no longer wanted to be a part of this wretched world where Iosif's violin no longer had a voice.

————

STRINGS SLOWLY GAVE WAY TO A MELANCHOLY OBOE, CALLING to Pyotr in B-flat minor. It was the opening of the second movement of his Fourth Symphony. The one he dedicated to dearest, *dearest* Nadezhda.

Was she singing to him as life seeped from his body?

"Petya," a voice sang in his ear. The music stopped. "Galina von Meck is here to play for you. Do you wish her to continue?"

Pyotr could not summon the strength to crack his eyes. All he could manage was to let his head drop slightly and then with all the heavenly willpower he could muster, raise it back up ever so little.

"Yes," he heard his brother speak. "Keep playing. He's been calling for your mother the past few days. Please, continue."

The mournful voice of the oboe began again. It lifted Pyotr from the bed until he floated weightless and serene above it. "You feel nostalgic for the past," he had told Nadezhda. "Yet with no compulsion to start life over again. Life has wearied you. It is time to pause, to weigh things up."

As the music continued, the heartache of the oboe became unbearable. He dropped like a slab of granite back onto the bed.

The music stopped.

His eyes flashed open and he gasped. "Nadezhda! *Why?* Why did you forsake me?"

Pyotr stared at the young woman who returned his gaze, her fingers still positioned over the keys of the oboe.

"I wanted only... only to kiss her hand!" he cried. Nadezhda's sudden rejection after so many years of communion – their minds intertwined through the exchange of thousands upon thousands of words on paper, haunted him mercilessly.

"I will never forget her," he sobbed. "Never! When I close my eyes she is there. If she suffers... I suffer with her."

The woman reached for Pyotr and touched his cheek. "My mother's fortune is gone. She is dying of tuberculosis in France. I'm leaving tomorrow to be with her," Galina said in a soothing voice. "But please, please know that your music beats in her heart."

"Only my music?" he croaked.

Galina pressed her warm hand against his cold cheek. "No, Pyotr Ilyich. She loves you." Galina lifted her hand and hung her head. "And I fear she will not endure very long after you are gone."

———

ОНА ЛЮБИТ ТЕБЯ.

"She loves you."

Она не выдержит долго после того, как ты уйдешь.

"She will not endure very long after you are gone."

The heartfelt voice of a woman speaking Russian.

она любит тебя.

"She loves you."

Suddenly he was back in New York, in his hotel suite talking with a reporter during his only visit to America a few years ago.

She was a reporter for the *Russian Gazette* and the *Northern Herald*. Her elegant Russian voice and her tender manner overwhelmed him.

"You are greatly admired here in America," she said.

As friendly and welcoming as his American hosts were, English was a strange language to his ears. Its vocabulary seemed to be composed of randomly plucked words from French and German. His mother tongue was so much purer, and connected directly to his soul.

He tried to stay focussed as she continued to probe. "And yet in Russia, there are many who scorn you still."

She paused a moment, locking eyes with him. Why did she seem to so embody his dear Nadezhda? Or his sister Alexandra who died last month, just a few days before he was to set sail for nine horrible days crossing the angry North Atlantic?

The young reporter leaned closer. In her eyes he saw a reflection of home. "And am I correct, yesterday was your birthday?"

Pyotr nodded. "Yes. Fifty-one."

"No!" the reporter smiled. "Someone said you were sixty, but I thought you much, much younger. The happiest of birthdays, sir!"

There was something about her Russian voice, delicate and nuanced, complex yet familiar. He trembled. His eyes glistened.

"Maestro?" she asked gently. "Is something troubling you? I am such an admirer of your music. It is a great honour to finally meet you and to be able write about how you so magnificently represent our country. Russia should be proud of such a talented son."

"Thank you, madam," he replied, his voice shaking.

He began to sob. His little sister was gone. Nadezhda had stopped writing to him. Mother Russia cared not, even if the New World was charmed. Were these Americans praising a fraud – a trickster with a handful of tuneful melodies?

"I'm sorry," he cried and ran into the adjacent bedroom, closing the door behind him and leaving the bewildered reporter sitting alone and bewildered. He fell onto his bed, sobbing uncontrollably. Despite his embarrassment, he cried until the pillow was wet with his tears.

A few minutes later he heard the door to his suite close. The reporter had left.

Burning with shame, he prayed she might be forgiving in reporting the rudeness of his behaviour.

Was New York just a dream?

Or was he really sitting across from a multi-millionaire – a little grey-bearded man so terribly indebted to Pyotr for sailing to America to help open his new music theatre a few days ago?

"I can't thank you enough for leaving Moscow to be here on opening night with us," Andrew Carnegie gushed with a tone of giddy reverence. "Your music was the first ever heard in Carnegie Hall!"

Walter Damrosch, a distinguished, well-groomed American conductor sitting at the dining room table with them coughed. His brow furrowed.

Carnegie glanced over and chuckled. "Oh, yes, yes, Walter, he followed your Beethoven overture," Andrew shot at Damrosch. "But Mr. Tchaikovsky was the first composer to conduct his own music in my wee hall."

Pyotr smiled. "With room for but a mere five thousand souls."

"Aye!" Andrew exclaimed. "And your music delighted every single one of them." His eyes danced to some inner joy. "We need to celebrate!"

They sat in Walter's dining room, while the ladies all occupied the parlour. Andrew nodded to the manservant attending them, who immediately exited the room and returned with a bottle of champagne. It was loudly uncorked and poured, bubbling into three tall flutes.

"A toast to my dear friend, Mr. Pyotr Tchaikovsky!" Andrew pronounced, holding his glass high in the air. "I adore Moscow. But I love your music even more, old man!"

"Thank you," Pyotr replied a little sheepishly. "Sir, I should point out that I only turned fifty-one yesterday."

"What?" Walter exclaimed. "Carnegie told me you were pushing sixty-five!"

Had he grown to look so old recently? Here he was being toasted by one of the richest men in the world, and yet he felt as poor and feeble as a dying peasant.

"Well, Happy Birthday, *young* man!" Andrew laughed. "You and I are going to do great things in America!"

They clinked their glasses together and drank the chilled champagne. It lifted Pyotr's spirits only a little. But Andrew was relentless in his ambitions for Pyotr.

"You need to come to New York every year, on your birthday if you wish. We'll stage your symphonies, your operas and maybe even..." he hesitated, "a ballet? Didn't I read that *Swan Lake* sold out at the Bolshoi for every single performance?"

Pyotr flushed with embarrassment. "Regardless. It received mixed reviews at best."

"Nonsense!" Andrew thundered. "And am I correct you wrote another ballet, *The Sleeping Beauty?*"

"Yes, but.."

Andrew Carnegie was fired up. Pyotr was taken not only with the man's energy, but how well read and literary he was, writing essays and books, befriending authors, poets and now it would seem, musical composers.

"What are you working on now?" Andrew pressed.

The man was incorrigible. "Actually, a new ballet. *The Nutcracker.*"

Andrew looked confused.

"It's a... well, I describe it as a sort of Christmas fairytale ballet," Pyotr explained. "The story is by a German, er, Prussian really, Hoffmann? But I'm working from the French adaptation by Dumas. It's going to be quite different than anything I've ever done."

"Different?" Walter, the conductor, repeated. "Different... how?"

Pyotr looked away a moment. He should be working on this new commission for the Imperial Theatre in Petersburg, but this trip to America had interrupted his work. He turned back to Andrew and Walter.

"Well, for a few scenes I want to use children's instruments – a little trumpet, a cuckoo, a rattle, drums, cymbals. Whatever my publisher can find for me."

"A Christmas fairy tale ballet with children's instruments?" Andrew repeated thoughtfully. "And a full orchestra too?"

"Of course," Pyotr replied. "I'm searching for something new, a kind of divinely unusual sound." He looked down. "But of course, it might all just be a grand flop."

"No, no!" Andrew countered with a booming confidence Pyotr found intimidating. "If I ever have children, I'm taking them to see *The Nutcracker* every Christmas."

Walter grunted, shaking his head. Pyotr shared his doubt

about the new work. The whole idea was rather too fanciful. The critics would likely savage it.

When the evening was finally over, with Carnegie going on and on about plans to give away his fortune so he would not die "rich and disgraced" Pyotr was exhausted.

Carnegie ordered his carriage to take Pyotr back to his hotel. On the way, Pyotr reflected on why everyone thought him such an old man. Probably because that was exactly how he looked.

Everything within him was falling apart.

In bed that night, thinking of how ancient and brittle he was, Pyotr fell into a restless sleep filled with horrible dreams. He was tumbling, falling uncontrollably down the face of a cliff into a black, angry sea. He clung desperately to a tiny ledge, about to fall to his death.

He was older at fifty-one than most men at ninety-one.

How much longer could he escape the waiting reaper?

Who were all these people and what did they want of him?

Pyotr opened his eyes and stared blankly at the ghostly figures gathered around his bed. A devil or perhaps a priest? Papa or...

"*Petya,*" a voice spoke. "Confess your sins, before your creator..." The voice paused, the speaker's warm breath very close, "please *Petya.* Your time is almost here."

He could not answer this plea for salvation. God's soldiers floated about, inky and transparent. Something was burning, smoking odours lingering heavy.

"Do you know who is here with you?" the voice asked. "It is us, your brothers, Modeste and Nicholas and your nephews, Litke, Buxhövden, and Vladimir."

"*Bobik?*" Pyotr mouthed faintly.

The face leaned in close. "I'm here, *dyadya*." Soft hands touched Pyotr's cheeks. "Please Uncle, be strong."

The words were meaningless as they fell upon Pyotr. Instead, a chorus of voices, crashing cymbals, a dark cello and finally a sweet clarinet bounced about freely inside his mind. How could he harmonize all these?

A picture filled his mind. He gripped the conductor's baton tightly, organizing the sounds of the orchestra as they began to play his last symphony, *Pathetique*. A farewell to everything and everyone he ever cared about. As the final haunting notes echoed through the grand hall, he slowly lowered his hand.

There was no applause. Only dead silence broken by muffled sobs and distant crying. The audience sat stunned. He stood before them and dropped his head until he heard a thunderous applause rising to Heaven.

A great heaviness suddenly overcame him, impossibly heavy, crushing him into a bed of stone until there was only nothingness.

Pyotr opened his eyes.

His brother Modest stared blankly. Behind him, brother Nicholas and dear, dear nephew *Bobik*, with all the kindness the world had to offer, stood slouching, eyes wet.

"Thank you, everyone," Pyotr spoke in a surprisingly firm tone. "I did not deserve your love. Please, forgive me for all the ways I wronged you."

"No!" Modeste cried. "You have nothing to..."

"Modi," Pyotr interrupted, looking through his brother into the beckoning eyes of the waiting universe. "I must go now."

MODEST TCHAIKOVSKY LET HIS HEAD DROP TO HIS CHEST. THE room fell silent.

Pyotr was gone.

His brother's suffering was over and if there be a merciful

God, Paradise had just welcomed a most gifted member to its musical elite.

A doctor traced his hands over Pyotr's eyelids, closing them forever. "Fifteen minutes after three o'clock in the morning," he called to another doctor taking notes. "Twenty-Five October, Eighteen Ninety-Three."

Modest was too drained to feel anything. But the quiet despair in his crowded little Petersburg flat was heavy. The doctors, the priest, his brother Nicholas and their three nephews all stood staring at the corpse laying still on the tiny bed.

The silence was punctuated with halting sobs from young nephew Vladimir, who Pyotr had called 'Bobik' since he was a baby. The second son of dearly departed sister Sasha, Bobik was now over twenty years old.

He dropped to his knees in front of the body. Sobbing, he leaned closer to Pyotr's pale, grey-bearded face to plant a kiss.

Modest held him back. "No. You must not touch him."

One of the doctors stepped forward. "The cholera is no longer a threat, Modest..." he hesitated, "but, we should still be careful. Are you going to call the undertaker? Or..."

Undertaker?

Modest glanced at his brother Nicholas who shook his head. Young Bobik, still on his knees in front of Pyotr's lifeless form, looked up. "No, Uncle!"

There would likely be many other who also wanted to pay respects. "We'll wait," Modest replied softly. "Until I can make arrangements."

"In that case," the doctor replied, "you should cover his face." He reached into his leather bag and produced a glass container. "And use this acid, carbolic, to swab his lips and his nostrils. Keep him disinfected if someone touches him."

The doctor handed the bottle to Modest. With that, the doctors packed up, as did the priest after saying a short prayer. Shortly afterwards Modest found himself alone with Pyotr. His brother and nephews were curled in sleep in the corners of his flat, but Modest remained teetering above the corpse, his thoughts and emotions jumbled.

"If only you knew, *Petya*," he whispered, "how great was your gift."

THE SEALED COFFIN SITTING AT THE ALTAR OF KAZAN Cathedral was surrounded by the largest sea of flowers and wreaths that Modest had ever seen.

He glanced back at the eight thousand faces crammed into a space designed for half as many. How they had been chosen from the sixty thousand who applied for tickets in the three days since his brother died, he did not know. Regardless, he could feel the love and admiration of each person behind him.

It was like a warm blanket against the chill of death.

The solemn service was punctuated with sobbing. When Modest rose with everyone else to sing 'We Hymn Thee' from the liturgy Pyotr composed more than a decade earlier, the many voices filled the cathedral as a single cry of despair from a grieving country.

Outside the cathedral, thousands more waited to join the procession to Tikhvin Cemetery. The Emperor himself was footing the cost and had helped organize the service. Modest could scarcely believe the outpouring of emotion coming from all corners of the country – delegations, tributes... honours of all sorts that would have overwhelmed his poor brother who so often preferred solitude.

But he would have loved the way his music resonated through the stone building. The pillars of granite topped with intricate gold carvings, the faces of saints painted on frescos high above, carved into the dome reaching for Heaven, seemed made for this moment. There was quiet shuffling across the floor of the marbled hall, but all were silent, waiting. A group of musicians were about to begin the final tribute from Pyotr's final symphony.

Modest had suggested the title '*Paticheskaya*' to describe the most passionate, emotional music his brother had ever composed. Pyotr concurred with the title, even though the publisher preferred the French translation, *Pathétique*. And remarkably, his brother did not disparage the work, but claimed it was his finest composition. He dedicated it to Bobik to whom Modest was surprised to learn yesterday Pyotr had bequeathed the rights to all his music.

The violins began with the slow finale in B minor. Modest felt his brother in this holy place as low notes from the cellos, the basses and bassoon repeated the opening themes. A more mournful masterpiece he could not recall. A more fitting sound for a funeral mass impossible to imagine.

The music ended *morendo*, the final movement fading out ever so slowly until all that was left was the echo of greatness.

THE END

EPILOGUE

Duscsting his brief fifty-three year odyssey on the planet, Pyotr Tchaikovsky left the world an abundance of musical treasurers, some which would take decades to permeate the consciousness of Western culture.

Two of his ballets, *The Nutcracker* and *Swan Lake*, remain the most often performed productions of professional ballet companies around the world. *The Nutcracker* alone generates forty percent of the revenue for many companies, while the world's top ballerinas receive more than $30,000 to dance a single performance of *Swan Lake*.

Yet for music critics, the very popularity and ubiquity of his works continues to detract from his standing. This is particularly true for his ballets, but also for the *1812 Overture, Romeo and Juliet*, the *Manfred Symphony, Francesca da Rimini*, the *Capriccio Italien* and the *Serenade for Strings*. His music is widely used in film and television productions, video games, advertisements, and social media creations, much to the consternation of serious classical music professionals who are quick to deride him to this day.

For the general public though, Tchaikovsky's music has remained popular around the world, second only to Beethoven amongst classical music composers. In Russia, he is a beloved composer generating national pride, even if the government continues to deny his homosexuality.

While we have presented glimpses into his life and music, there is so much more that could be written about him. Entire websites are devoted to his letters, diaries, music and the people in his life. Treatises on his death, his sexual preferences, his correspondence with Nadezhda von Meck, and of course his music, fill many corners of the internet. There is also no shortage of books, journals, documentaries, and fictional films analyzing every aspect of his life.

Though the discipline of theoretical analysis can be a useful tool in vivisecting a musical piece, the true worth of an opus can only be understood by experiencing its performance. In today's world of streaming digital services, these performances are at one's fingertips, and we sincerely hope that the observations and commentaries from previous chapters inspire you to explore the oeuvre of Tchaikovsky further, thus experiencing the gifts of this amazing composer for themselves.

A FINAL WORD

FOR SOMEONE SO INSECURE ABOUT HIS MUSIC AND HIS relations with others, often struggling with demons of his own creation, Pyotr never stopped composing, working right up until the last few weeks of his life. He was an extremely articulate man and respected by other composers, the giants of his time, and although often plagued by fierce critics, he left the world with an enormous catalogue of music. His lifetime of work includes seven symphonies, ten operas, three ballets, numerous suites, overtures, piano and violin concertos, cantatas, choral works, string quartets, and over one hundred songs and piano pieces.

And when he died, he was considered to be at the height of

his compositional prowess. Yet for all he accomplished and the musical gifts he bestowed upon the world, the true inner life of this man remains something of which we can only speculate.

And remain in eternal wonder of the music he left behind.

ABOUT THE AUTHORS

Steve Moretti is a writer and music lover from Ottawa, Canada. His first novel and audiobook series, *Song for a Lost Kingdom,* is powered by an ancient cello that connects two composers across time. He has a passion for history and time-travel and is currently at work on a new series entitled *Michael Angelo.*

Paul van Geldrop is a voice actor and composer from the Netherlands. His passion for music extends to both the practical and theoretical sides, be it composing his own work or studying the works of others. He is currently pursuing a Master's degree in Orchestration.

PLEASE LEAVE A REVIEW!

*Unbearable crap
from start to finish
cse level drivel !*

If you enjoyed *Pyotr*, please take a moment to leave us a short review or rating. Your honest opinion is valuable to other readers.

You can leave a review on Amazon, Goodreads or BookBub.

Thank you!

Steve Moretti
Paul van Geldrop

SONG FOR A LOST KINGDOM SERIES
BY STEVE MORETTI

The Prequel: *A Kingdom is Lost, A Song is Born* eBook, Audiobook

Book I: *Music is Not Bound by Time* eBook, Paperback, Audiobook

Book II: *Love Never Surrenders* eBook, Paperback, Audiobook

Book III: *The Heart Beats in Time* eBook, Paperback, Audiobook,

SFLK Box Set - *4 Book set plus bonus goodies*

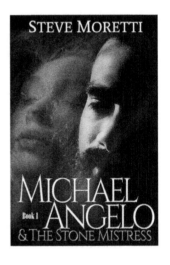

SEVEN DEADLY PENS
THRILLER, FANTASY AND MYSTERY STORIES TO KEEP YOU UP ALL NIGHT

Turn the lights down low, make a cup of your favourite brew and get tucked in for seven page-turning short stories. The collection includes thriller, mystery, science fiction and fantasy tales, all with deadly consequences. Available now.

Andy and the Time Slip App
by Steve Moretti

Andy had a very good life until temptation got the best of him one day. But if he can rewind time, is he free to break the rules again?

Also includes stories from K. Bradley, David Devine, Matt C. Sully, Lara Bujold Clouden, Peter Smith and Merja Tammi.